W9-CEZ-895

Disabled Workers in the Labor Market

This study was conducted by The Bureau of Applied Social Research of Columbia University with the cooperation of the Vocational Rehabilitation Administration of the United States Department of Health, Education, and Welfare.

DISABLED WORKERS IN THE LABOR MARKET

A. J. JAFFE
LINCOLN H. DAY
WALTER ADAMS

THE BEDMINSTER PRESS

Copyright © 1964, The Bedminster Press, Totowa, N. J.

PRINTED IN THE UNITED STATES OF AMERICA

Library of Congress Catalogue Card Number 63-18086

Readers of this book are invited to send name and address to THE BEDMINSTER PRESS, *Vreeland Avenue, Totowa, New Jersey, U.S.A., to receive announcements and literature about other books in the social sciences published by* THE BEDMINSTER PRESS.

Contents

vi

Charts

Preface

The major purpose of this study is to ascertain the position in the labor market of seriously and permanently disabled men, following their injury. How do these men fare? Do they all become chronically unemployed? Are they uniformly turned down by personnel men when they apply for jobs? Or do they all make suitable adjustments, so that they are fully employed to the extent of their capabilities? Obviously the truth, insofar as it can be ascertained, must lie somewhere between these two extremes. But where? We emphasize this question, since employment agencies concerned with finding jobs for the disabled have reported difficulties in doing so, and personnel men, when interviewed, often appear reluctant to hire them. Hence, only by actually ascertaining the employment and unemployment experiences of these men can we determine what has happened—and is now happening—to them.

Obtaining a reasonably adequate cross section of all seriously and permanently disabled men is difficult. A practical approach is to work with a group of men who have been injured on the job and therefore are known to the workmen's compensation boards. This was done. We can assume that the experiences of such men are probably little different from those of men who have been seriously and permanently disabled by non-job accidents or incidents—such as adult polio victims, men in traffic accidents while on vacation, etc. On the other hand, men with congenital disabilities, or men who were injured during war, may have quite different employment experiences. Nevertheless, we have confidence that our findings can be generally applied to other men who had some work experience before becoming permanently and seriously disabled.

Given the intent of our study and the reason for selecting workmen's compensation cases for study, it follows that we are *not* investigating any workmen's compensation or vocational rehabilitation system. Indeed, even if we wanted to do so, our data do not permit passing any judgement on the efficiency of these systems. This is because our cases were taken from three jurisdictions: State of New Jersey; New York State; and that of the Federal government covering Federal employees, longshoremen and harbor workers. We do not have enough cases from any one jurisdiction to analyze it separately. We have, instead, a reasonably good cross section of the New York metropolitan area, and we are reporting here about this totality.

Now any group of men will contain some who were more, and some who were less, successful as far as their employment histories and experiences are concerned. Accordingly, our analysis is basically divided into two main parts: 1) describing and comparing men who were successfully employed, following their workmen's compensation injury, and those who were not so employed; and 2) trying to predict, on the basis of the information known about the injured man as of the time of his accident, how successful his subsequent employment history was likely to be. The remaining materials, in large measure, are supplementary to these two main parts.

Part I, *Employment Status of the Disabled Men,* contains a comparison of the men who, at the time of interview (approximately five years after the accident which brought them into our study), were successfully employed and those who were not. "Successful" employment is measured in two ways: a) being employed at the time of interview (or not being employed); and b) by the amount and quality of employment which the man had in the year preceding the interview.

Part II, *Attempts to Predict Future Experiences in the Labor Market* does exactly that. One of the main purposes of such attempts is to select out as early as possible those men who, if left to their own devices entirely, would be failures in the job market. These are the men who need help, call it vocational rehabilitation or what you will. If they can be detected early enough, presumably more of them can be brought around to the point where they will be successfully employed.

Part III, *Job Training, Job Adjustments, and Job Seeking* describes the various steps taken by the men when they returned—or attempted to return—to work. In Part IV, *Men Out of Work,* description is presented of those who, at the time of interview, were job "failures." Also present-

xii

ed here is a brief picture of the financial support available to these men when out of work because of disability.

The Appendixes contain certain supplementary materials which we believe are very pertinent to the main body of our findings. We wish to call the reader's attention in particular to Appendixes B, C, and D, which present additional quantitative materials on the prevalence of accidents. In Appendix B are presented some previously unpublished data from the United States National Health Survey, and in Appendixes C and D additional calculations, derived from the workmen's compensation data and from our interviews, on the probability of a man's having a serious disabling work injury, and on the probability of his having a second injury.

A note on our analytical methods is pertinent at this point. For the most part we have made our analysis, and based our conclusions, on cross-tabulations of the data and comparisons of one group with another. To the extent that two groups differ with respect to employment, we draw inferences concerning the distinguishing characteristic only when relevant. For example, comparison of the employment situation of younger and older men will provide information on the possible relevancy of age to employment. Wherever such comparisons were made, conclusions have been drawn and presented only where the differences were statistically significant. Generally, where no statistically significant differences appeared, we omitted such findings from the analysis.

As happens with virtually all surveys, the number of interviews obtained—no matter how large the number may be—is always too small to provide the most meaningful and statistically significant analyses. Too many insights and "ideas" turn out to be statistically chance results because of the small numbers of cases. Our study is no different. Therefore, in order to expedite matters we have simply omitted all "findings" which are not statistically reliable.

Finally we wish to acknowledge our debt to the many people who assisted us in one way or another on this study. Dr. Isidore Lubin, formerly Industrial Commissioner for New York State, Mr. William B. Folger, Executive Director of the New York State Insurance Fund, and Mr. Theodore Hetzler of the National Association of Mutual Casualty Companies, encouraged us greatly at the inception of this study; indeed, without their aid we should never have gotten started. We wish to thank for their cooperation: Mr. Arnold Quigley and Mr. Thomas P. Esmonde of the United States Bureau of Employees' Compensation; Mr. Thomas Franklin, Chief of the New Jersey Division of Workmen's Compensation; Mr. S. E. Senior, who is the Chairman, and Mr. Jacob Schutzbank of the New York State Workmen's Compensation Board; Mr. Willis Gorthy, late Director of the Institute for the Crippled and Disabled, New York City; Dr. Henry H. Kessler of the Kessler Institute for Rehabilitation, West Orange, New Jersey; and Dr. A. David Gurewitsch. Mr. W. Granville Lee of the New York State Workmen's Compensation Board, Mr. Joseph J. Agresto of the United States Bureau of Employees' Compensation, and Mr. Walt R. Simmons of the U.S. National Health Survey very kindly furnished us with various statistical data necessary for the conduct of this study. Three others who helped greatly in carrying on the work were J. Ronald Milavsky, Barry Pollack, and Philip Springer, all of Columbia University.

We are grateful for the interest and help of Mrs. Eleanor Roosevelt, who not only wrote at length of our project in her *New York Post* column, but also permitted us to use a letter of hers addressed to the respondents to assist in obtaining interviews. Because of her generous assistance the responses to our requests for interviews were very substantially increased.

Dr. Robert C. Darling gave us consistently good advice on medical and other aspects of our study, and commented upon an earlier draft of the manuscript. Dr. Lazare Teper also read and commented upon the manuscript. We benefited from all this advice, we hope. But we alone are responsible for the contents and conclusions presented here.

xiv

Disabled Workers in the Labor Market

[1]

Introduction

Certain groups of workers are advantageously situated with respect to employment opportunities. Formally or informally, such characteristics as age, sex, schooling, physique, race, etc., are often taken into consideration by the prospective employer. As a result, various fair employment practices acts have been passed which try to provide equal employment opportunities for all groups of workers. Despite such laws, some workers still appear to be actually, or potentially, at a disadvantage in the employment market.

The focus of this study comprises the job experiences of one such potentially disadvantaged group: selected men in the New York metropolitan area who had become seriously, permanently disabled in the course of their employment.[1] In order to come within the limits of our sample of this group, the disabled man had to have been employed, and seriously, permanently injured in the course of that employment. Thus, our study excluded not only women and the self-employed, but also that unknown number of men so disabled from birth or from childhood injuries and illnesses that they never enter the labor force or, at best, remain in it only very marginally. In addition, it excluded that other group of the disabled made up of persons whose disabilities have arisen from non-job activities: war, off-the-job automobile accidents, and so forth.

What happens to that group of persons included in this study is no small matter, however, despite these exclusions. Of the 65 million work-

---

[1] See following section on "Universe."

1

ers in the United States in 1959, including the self-employed, two million experienced death or disability that year as the result of conditions arising out of their employment. We define "disabling injuries" as those which disable the worker beyond the day of accident. During the ten years of the 1950s, over 145,000 workers were killed on the job and another 19.5 million suffered disabling injuries.[2] That this represents some improvement over the previous decade is, of course, of scant comfort to those involved, whether directly or indirectly.

Aside from occasioning pain, disablement and death, work injuries are also the cause of considerable financial loss to the worker. The National Safety Council estimates wage losses from this source in 1959 at $4.2 billion.[3] Even if we assume that none of the monies received under workmen's compensation were intended to compensate in any way for either pain or disability—that, in other words, everything received was as compensation solely for loss of income—workmen's compensation *still* made up for only an estimated 60 per cent of the 1959 loss in wages arising from work injuries.[4] And taking into consideration the effect of price changes and losses in legal fees, we can conclude that this proportion over the last decade or two has actually amounted to no more than a third.[5]

The social, economic, medical, and employment problems that arise as a result of job-connected accidents are extensive and affect large numbers of workers and their families. They have called forth great efforts in an attempt to provide solutions—improved medical care, vocational rehabilitation, special efforts to find jobs for the permanently disabled, workmen's compensaion payments, safety laws, factory inspection. Any such preventive, ameliorative, or curative program will be successful to the extent that it is based on the maximum factual knowledge of the problems faced. Accordingly, we believe that any additional information to be gained regarding the characteristics of persons injured on the job, the circumstances under which they are injured, their post-accident experiences, and the characteristics of the jobs involved in these

---

2 National Safety Council, *Accident Facts, 1960 Edition*, pp. 22, 23.

3 *Ibid.*, p. 24.

4 *Ibid.*, p. 35.

5 Herman M. Somers and Anne Ramsey Somers, *Workmen's Compensation*, N. Y. John Wiley and Sons, 1954, pp. 12, 81.

2

injuries, will be useful in the further development of any programs aimed at coping with job-connected injuries and their aftermath.

THE UNIVERSE

Criteria for Inclusion in Study

The material presented in this report combines information from workmen's compensation records and interviews with more than a thousand disabled men in the New York area. The characteristics of our universe are discussed in more detail in Appendix A, "Methodology." Suffice it to say here that it consisted of men who were (1) less than 60 years old in 1960; (2) recipients of workmen's compensation for serious, permanent disablement; (3) resident in the New York Metropolitan Area both at the time of the injury and at the time of interview; (4) not involved in any workmen's compensation litigation or third-party suits at the time of interview; and (5) injured between January 1, 1950, and September 30, 1957.

The decision as to whether a man was permanently disabled was left to the respective workmen's compensation boards—those of the states of New Jersey and New York, and of the Federal government. A board's decision that a disability was permanent qualified the man for our study —if that disability were also "serious enough." For purposes of our study, the criterion for minimum severity was defined as a disability equal to the total loss of a thumb. Such a loss entitles the worker to 75 weeks of compensation under the Federal system, and also under that of each of the two states (New York and New Jersey) with jurisdiction in the New York metropolitan area. It is a serious loss and, on the basis of schedules used by these compensation boards, is equivalent to a loss of about 25 per cent of the use of a hand, or 36 per cent of the use of a foot.

We did, however, check each individual's account of his current condition, and removed from our tabulations those who reported no disability at all, and also those whose disabilities were patently trivial. The latter group of "rejects" was composed primarily of "facials," recipients of awards of between $500 and $1000.

Age and Education of Men in Population

As a result of applying the above criteria, we obtained few men under age 25 and no men above age 60, as of 1960. The omission of younger

3

men results simply from the fact that the injuries had occurred in the early or middle 1950s when the men were, on the average, about five years younger than at the time of interview. Men aged 60 and over were deliberately excluded. The age distribution of the disabled men then compares with all employed men in the New York Metropolitan Area[6] (in 1960) as follows:

Age	All men		Disabled men	
14 years to 29 years	21%		7%	
30 years to 34 years	12		9	
35 years to 44 years	24		34	
Under age 45		57		50
45 years to 54 years	22		41	
55 and over	21		9	
Age 45 and over		43		50
All ages		**100%**		**100%**

The educational level of the disabled men was below that of all men aged 25 to 54 years living in the New York Metropolitan Area[7]:

Years of schooling	All men	Disabled men
8 years or less	23%	36%
9 to 11 years	23	30
12 years, high school grad.	37	22
1 or more years of college	17	12
Total	**100%**	**100%**

THE WORKMEN'S COMPENSATION SYSTEMS

A knowledge of the main features of the three workmen's compensation programs applicable to workers in the New York area (the New York, New Jersey, and Federal systems) is important to an understanding of the nature of our universe and the character of our findings. Not only did we choose our universe from among men who had received some form of workmen's compensation; we also, in our selection, accepted the determination of the workmen's compensation boards concerning the permanency and severity of individual disabilities, with the exceptions already noted.

The first workmen's compensation law in the United States was passed in 1908. It covered only civil employees of the Federal Government.

---

[6] U. S. Census of Population, 1960, *New York*, "Detailed Characteristics," PC(1) 34D, Table 123.

[7] *Ibid.*, Table 103.

4

Three years later, ten states passed such legislation, to be followed within the next decade by all but six of the remaining states. With passage of the last workmen's compensation law in 1948, the system was extended to every state in the Union.

> "The main purpose of workmen's compensation laws was to eliminate the uncertainties of getting damages for injuries at common law or under employers' liability laws. Before workmen's compensation laws were adopted, the employee who was injured on his job got little or nothing in recompense. To recover damages against his employer he had to file suit and to prove that the injury was due to the employer's negligence. The employer, even though he had been negligent, could avail himself of three common law defenses: "assumption of risk," "fellow servant rule," and "contributory negligence." That is, the employer could defeat recovery if it was proved that the employee's injury was due to ordinary risks of his work, if it was caused by the negligence of a fellow worker, or if the employee by his own negligence in any way contributed to the injury."[8]

Today there are in the United States 53 separate workmen's compensation laws: 51 for individual states and the District of Columbia and two for Federal jurisdictions (Federal employees, and longshore and harbor workers).[9] Though similar in general outline, no two of the laws are exactly alike. The variation between them is enormous—in the extent to which coverage is compulsory, the kinds of employment excluded from coverage, the definition of a "compensable injury," coverage for occupational disease, whether or not a waiting period is required, maximum amounts payable, the extent to which medical care is furnished, the use of lump sum awards, the possibilities for vocational and physical rehabilitation. In general, agricultural workers, domestics, and "casual" workers are not covered, and nearly half the jurisdictions exempt firms with fewer than three employees. The result is that approximately one out of five workers in this country receives no coverage at all, a proportion higher in some states than in others.[9a]

By almost any criterion, the program for Federal employees is the

---

[8] "State Workmen's Compensation Laws," Bulletin No. 161, revised, U. S. Department of Labor, Bureau of Labor Standards, May 1960, p. 1. See also the Supplement to Bulletin No. 161, issued December 1961.

[9] Maritime workers and railroad employees in interstate commerce are covered under two other systems, the Jones Act and the Federal Employers' Liability Act, respectively.

[9a] See the excellent article by Alfred M. Skolnik, "New Benchmarks in Workmen's Compensation," *Social Security Bulletin*, June 1962, pp. 5-7.

most liberal and that for longshore and harbor workers only somewhat less so. Of the state programs, New York's is certainly one of the more liberal. The following chart summarizes the main features of these four workmen's compensation systems *for the years when the men in our universe received their disabling injuries.*

It should be emphasized that these are the features of the four workmen's compensation systems that apply in the area of our research during the years when the men in our universe received their disabling injuries. There have been several changes since then: for example, the maximum weekly award in 1963 is $55 in New York, and in New Jersey for permanent total disability, $45. But because these provisions for increased benefits are not retroactive, the men whom we studied have been unable to take advantage of them. For them, these provisions remain as they were at the time they were injured.

SUMMARY GROUPS AND INDEXES DESIGNED FOR OUR ANALYSIS

Much of our analysis centers about a number of summary groups and indexes, each of which combines separate items of information about the respondents. These summaries are of two main types: (1) those concerned with experience in the labor market, and (2) those concerned with certain variables thought to influence the character of that experience. Some of these indexes will be fully described at appropriate places in the text. Where this is the case, only brief mention will be made of them here. The others we shall discuss more fully.

The major summary groups and indexes are as follows:

A—Labor Performance Summary Groups

B—Indexes of Factors Influencing Experience in the Labor Market

1. Physical Index
2. Emotional Index
3. Socializing Index
4. Summary Index
5. Injury Summaries

Labor Performance Summary Groups

We identified three labor performance groups: men with "better" jobs; men with "same or somewhat poorer" jobs; and men with "very poor or no" jobs. Two primary criteria were used to place respondents in one or the other of these three categories: (1) direction and extent

6

of any wage change between the time of the most serious job-connected injury (or illness) since January, 1950, and the date of the interview; and (2) whether or not the respondent worked full time, part time, or not at all during the year preceding the interview.

We defined a respondent as having secured a wage gain if, at the time of interview, his weekly earnings were at least $10 higher than at the time of his most serious, job-connected injury. This figure of $10 is a conservative estimate of the increase a male worker in the New York area would have had to receive in order to keep abreast of wage changes over the period between injury and interview (averaging approximately five years). To be "full time," a respondent had to have worked at least 40 weeks in the year and for at least 35 hours per week. Persons who had both increased their wages by $10 or more and worked full time were defined as having "better" jobs. Those who had not gained at least $10, but had worked full time, were put into the "same or somewhat poorer" job category. Those who had not gained and also had not worked full time, or else had not worked at all, were classified as having a "very poor or no" job. The distribution by labor performance groups was as follows:

Labor Performance Summary Group	*Per cent*
Men with "better" jobs	41
Men with "same or somewhat poorer" jobs	39
Men with "very poor or no" jobs	20
Total:	**100**

Indexes of Factors Influencing Experience in the Labor Market

Physical Index. An attempt was made to gather, without benefit of a medical examination, some information on the current physical condition of each man in our study. Some of these data were derived from the respondent's own estimate of his condition; some from what we hoped was a reasonably factual, straightforward account of his injuries and illnesses; and two items were observations by the interviewer. From the combination of these various bits of information we constructed a Physical Index which we trusted would closely mirror the actual physical health and capacities of the respondents. In doing so, we were aware that it might also reflect somewhat the emotional aspects of physical complaints. The general procedure for developing the index was to test each separate item of information by comparing the two extreme labor performance summary groups: those with "better" jobs and those with

7

Disabled Workers in the Labor Market

WORKMEN'S COMPENSATION FOR THE PERMANENTLY DISABLE

System	Coverage compulsory to qualify for maximum weekly award	Employment excluded from coverage	Minimum no. of employees to qualify for compulsory coverage	Length of waiting period	Occupational diseases	Percentage ave weekly wage paid as awar
N. J.	No	All casual, most farm & domestic workers; maritime & rail workers engaged in any interstate trade	No numerical exceptions	7 days	Full coverage	66-2/3% but not above maximum
N. Y.	Yes	Most farm & domestic workers; maritime & rail workers engaged in any interstate trade	Two	7 days	Full coverage, except: benefits not paid for partial disability from silicosis and asbestosis	66-2/3% but not above maximum
Federal	Yes	None	No numerical exceptions	3 days	Full coverage	66-2/3% (75% if ed worker has tory dependen
L & Harbor Workers	Yes	None	No numerical exceptions	3 days	Full coverage	66-2/3% but not above maximum

SOURCES FOR CHART ON WORKMEN'S COMPENSATION PROVISIONS:
1. "State Workmen's Compensation Laws," Bulletin 161 (revised May 1960), U.S. Department of Labor, Bureau of Labor Standards, Government ing Office, 1960.
2. New York State, *Workmen's Compensation Law*, New York State Workmen's Compensation Board, September, 1957.
3. New York State, *Workmen's Compensation Law, 1958-1959 Supplement*, New York State Workmen's Compensation Board, May 15, 1959.

8

IROUGH JOB-INCURRED DISEASE OR INJURY, JAN. 1, 1950–SEPT. 30, 1957

ximum awards able per week	*Minimum weekly wage to qualify for maximum weekly award*	*Total maximum stated in law*	*Use of lump sum awards*	*Medical care*	*Provisions for rehabilitation*	*System*
cases in our uni- rse closed, '56) 'cases in our uni- rse closed, '58)	$45 (1956 closings) $60 (1958 closings)	None	When in "best inter- ests" of workers	Full benefits	Maximum $30 weekly, for "permanent to total" disability class only	**N. J.**
	$54	None	For all facial disfigure- ments; occasionally for other injuries (esp. backs and car- diac).	Full benefits	$20 weekly mainte- nance; additional amt. rehab. services	**N. Y.**
.15	$181.72	None	"If director determines it is in best interest of beneficiary"	Full benefits	Max. $50 month, main tenance; also pro- vides cost of rehab. service	**Federal**
up to 7.26.56; 4 after that date	$52.50 to 7.26.56; $81 after that date	None	If deputy commissioner determines it is "in the best interest of justice"	Full benefits	Max. $10 week main- tenance (to 7.26.56) $25 a week after that date	**L & Harbor Workers**

ate of New Jersey, *Workmen's Compensation Law Revised Statutes 1937, As Amended and Supplemented to January 1, 1957 with Additional Leg- ation, 1957.*
ngshoremen's and Harbor Workers' Compensation Act, as amended to July 26, 1956, Government Printing Office, 1958.
onroe Berkowitz, *Workmen's Compensation: The New Jersey Experience,* New Brunswick, N. J., 1960.
mers and Somers, *op. cit.*

"very poor or no" jobs. Seven items from the initial lengthy list both differentiated strongly these two groups and selected out a respectable percentage of one group or the other. The seven items, and the results obtained when tested on the two labor performance groups, appear in the following table:

Physical Indicators	*Per cent with positive mentions*		
	(A)	*(B)*	*Ratio:*
		Men with	
	Men with	*"very poor*	
	"better" jobs	*or no" jobs*	*(A) to (B)*
1. Ill or unable to work during year preceding interview	0.0	40.1	—
2. Unable to work at time of interview	0.0	23.1	—
3. Limited mobility at time of interview	5.8	42.0	1 to 7.2
4. Handicap extremely visible to interviewer	5.7	14.0	1 to 2.5
5. Current health "poor"	4.9	30.6	1 to 6.2
6. An injury cluster[a]	4.5	26.8	1 to 6.0
7. A post-1957 injury or illness[b]	11.5	39.7	1 to 3.5

  a Four or more injuries or illnesses since 1953, three or more since 1955, or two or more since 1957.
  b These men had at least two injuries, for, to be included in the universe, they also had to have been injured *before* October 1, 1957.

The seven items comprising the Physical Index appear to be of two general types: (1) indicators of objective impairment or limited function, or (2) indicators which, while failing to specify objective impairment or limited function in any explicit sense, do, nevertheless, denote an unfavorable physical condition or occurrence. The first four indicators in the table are of the first type; the last three of the second.

For purposes of analysis, men with affirmative mentions on one or more of the first four questions (whether or not any of the last three were also mentioned) formed one category on the final Physical Index; men with no mention of any of the first four, but with a mention of one or more of the last three, formed a second category; and persons with no mention of any of the seven indicators formed a third.[10] In the table

---

10 We did, however, identify the original seven indicators in a punch-card column, as follows: If a respondent had a mention of indicator (1) in the table, he was punched "1." If there was no mention of indicator (1), but a mention of indicator

which follows, these three categories are distributed among the three Labor Performance Summary Groups.

	Men with "better" jobs	Men with "same or somewhat poorer" jobs	Men with "very poor or no" jobs
Physical Index mention:	%	%	%
Objective impairment or limited function mentioned	10	17	57
Unfavorable physical mention; no objective impairment or limited function mentioned	15	14	21
No unfavorable physical mention of any sort	75	69	22
Total:	**100**	**100**	**100**

Emotional Index. Several questions were asked concerning attitudes and "self-images," in addition to several others concerning modes of living often associated with some degree of emotional deprivation (e.g., being unmarried and living alone[11]). It is unlikely that any of the variables with which we worked in our study can be understood in exclusively "physical" or "emotional" terms. Any "emotional index" is bound to reflect physical conditions to some extent—and vice versa. We can see in the following table, for example, that when asked about their present physical condition, men with a poor labor performance record subsequent to injury were far more likely than the others to *volunteer* a mention of their disabilities. This was true regardless of whether they defined their conditions as "good," "fair," or "poor." In all, we tested 15 possible emotional indicators to determine how they differentiated the two extreme labor performance groups: those with "better" and those with "very poor or no" jobs.

---

(2), he was punched "2," and so forth for all seven indicators. In short, we identified each respondent by whichever of his mentions had the highest priority—priority being given, first, to the indicators of objective impairment or limited function (which are, ostensibly, more relevant to work performance) and then, within each category, to those indicators found to be the more discriminating between the two extreme labor performance groups.

11 See Gurin, Veroff, and Feld, *Americans View Their Mental Health*, Ann Arbor, Survey Research Center, University of Michigan, 1961, p. 235 and pp. 368-369. Also see Stanley Schachter, *The Psychology of Affiliation*, Stanford, Stanford University Press, 1959.

Labor Performance Summary Group	Per cent voluntarily mentioning disability by own evaluation of health			
	Good health	*Fair health*	*Poor health*	*Total*
"Better" jobs	28	30	*	29
"Same or somewhat poorer" jobs	32	40	38	36
"Very poor or no" jobs	52	45	46	48

* Too few cases to permit showing percentage.

We finally selected for our index the five indicators in the following table:

	Per cent with positive mentions		
	(A) *Men with "better" jobs*	*(B)* *Men with "very poor or no" jobs*	*Ratio: (A) to (B)*
The respondent . . . said: in low or very low spirits most of the time.	5	21	1 to 4.2
said: in general preferred to be alone rather than with other people	9	19	1 to 2.1
volunteered mention of disability when asked of general health level; also said: often in pain (in answer to separate question).	11	27	1 to 2.5
said: had less good luck than most people.	16	39	1 to 2.4
was single person living alone at time of interview.	10	22	1 to 2.2

For our analysis we summarized the index as a simple dichotomy: those with one or more emotional mentions, and those with none. The distribution by labor performance is shown in the following table:

12

Emotional Index mention:	Men with "better" jobs %	Men with "same or somewhat poorer" jobs %	Men with "very poor or no" jobs %
Yes	34	44	69
No	66	56	31
Total:	**100**	**100**	**100**

Before closing our description of the Physical and Emotional Indexes, we should note that, of the items included in our questionnaire, only those mentioned in this discussion could have been tested, and then accepted or rejected, for the construction of such indexes. The questionnaire contained no others. A physician or psychiatrist examining each of the respondents individually might have arrived at a different conclusion. Unable to submit the men in our study to such an examination—yet desirous of some indication of general physical and emotional condition—we were forced to resort to questions that could be asked by interviewers untrained in either medicine or the study of mental health. The ones used were chosen after consultation with our medical advisor. We cannot defend our indexes as approximations of the diagnostic categories employed by physicians or psychiatrists. We do defend them, however, as general indicators of the physical and emotional state of the men. Most importantly, it is significant that these indicators discriminated between labor performance groups far better than many traditional measures of disability or health or injury commonly used in compensation systems, such as "location of injury," or "amount of award" (as based on medical examination of the injured person).

Socializing Index. We conceived of this Index as being an objective measure of gregariousness, excluding relationships within the family circle. Personal preference for being alone or with others was not included. It was already an element of the Emotional Index, and, in any case, told us nothing about actual behavior. Two additional questions are available for analysis: "About how often each month do you get together with your friends?" and "Since your injury, have you been able to be with other people as much as you would like?" We ended with three categories comprising the Socializing Index. They are distributed by labor performance groups in the following table:

13

Disabled Workers in the Labor Market

Socializing mention:	Men with "better" jobs %	Men with "same or somewhat poorer" jobs %	Men with "very poor or no" jobs %
A. Respondent sees friends less than once a month; this not as much as he would like	9	12	26
B. Respondent sees friends less than once a month; this as much as he would like	10	12	13
C. Respondent sees friends more than once a month.a	81	76	61
Total:	**100**	**100**	**100**

a For most analytic purposes we summarized in a simple dichotomy, category "A" versus "B & C."

Summary Index. In the early stages of our analysis we made some preliminary tabulations using the Physical, Emotional, and Socializing Indexes separately. But we soon determined that we needed a Summary Index that would combine these three. The scheme below indicates the twelve categories we identified in a punch-card column for each respondent:

	Mention on Physical Index		Mention on Emotional Index	Mention on Socializing Index
	Objective impairment or limited function	No objective impairment or limited function mentioned a		
1.	Yes	—	Yes	Yes
2.	No	Yes	Yes	Yes
3.	Yes	—	Yes	No
4.	No	Yes	Yes	No
5.	Yes	—	No	Yes
6.	No	Yes	No	Yes
7.	No	No	Yes	Yes
8.	No	No	Yes	No
9.	Yes	—	No	No
10.	No	Yes	No	No
11.	No	No	No	Yes
12.	No	No	No	No

a If the respondent had an objective impairment or reported limited function, we did not code any of the other physical indicators. These other physical indicators were coded only if the men had no indication of objective impairment or did not report limited function.

14

Cross-tabulating these twelve categories by labor performance groups yielded a 36-cell table. Quite clearly, this table had too few cases per cell for statistical reliability. In doing this, however, we noted that the Socializing Index, although it had discriminated well between labor performance groups, selected out the smallest proportion of any of the three indexes, and also selected almost no persons not already selected by the Emotional Index. Hence, so far as cross-tabulation with the Labor Performance Summary Groups was concerned, the Socializing Index could be eliminated, and the Emotional Index be understood virtually to stand for it.[12]

Mentions on Indexes	*"Better" jobs*	*"Same or poorer" jobs*	*"Very poor or no" jobs*
	%	%	%
Physical *and* emotional-socializing	11	18	59
Physical *only*	15	12	18
Emotional-social-izing *only*	23	27	10
No mentions	51	43	13
Total:	**100**	**100**	**100**

Injury Summaries

Our questionnaire attempted to record all major injuries and illnesses experienced during each respondent's lifetime, whether or not job-connected. We screened out the common childhood diseases, and also such common ones as Asian flu, unless serious and lengthy complications or a permanent disability had resulted from them. Common surgical procedures, such as tooth extractions and appendectomies, were handled in similar fashion. Our basic criteria for including an illness or injury episode were: (1) it had resulted in permanent disability; or (2) it resulted in at least one month's unemployment; or (3) it was the first episode in

---

12 We also noted that distinguishing: (1) objective impairment or limited function, and (2) physical mention without mention of (1) added little to the tabulation and that merging caused minor loss. The table is the most succinct version of the Summary Index, cross-tabulated by labor performance groups. We realize, of course, that on tabulations other than by labor performance the Socializing Index might prove independently significant. This could be true, since far more men mentioned emotional problems than mentioned both emotional and socializing ones. Those with emotional mentions only were distributed similarly to those with both for the labor performance groups, but might not distribute similarly for other variables.

Disabled Workers in the Labor Market

a related series (e.g., the first back injury in a series of three medically-related back injuries) which then, or later, met the requirements of (1) or (2) above; or (4) it was a later episode in a related series, temporally distinct from earlier episodes, and also adding a distinct increment to the disability. All episodes, then, were relatively serious, though some might be less so than the illness or injury that brought the respondent into the sample; an injury which was, by definition, permanently disabling. A possible source of some bias stems from the fact that more recent episodes of illness or injury were less likely to be forgotten and were, as a consequence, more fully represented in the interviews. There was no way of gauging the extent of this bias, however.

From this medical history we were able to develop two summaries, one indicating for each respondent the aggregate of injuries and illnesses (i.e., the sum of the episodes, each episode counted as one, regardless of its relation to any other episode). Secondly, we counted the number of episodes for each respondent, considering a related series of episodes as one only. The latter summary proved the more useful. The three categories we generally tabulated, which are here cross-tabulated with the Labor Performance Summary Groups, are presented in the following table:

	Men with "better" jobs %	Men with "same or somewhat poorer" jobs %	Men with "very poor or no" jobs %
One injury or illness only	48	39	29
Multiple injuries and/or illnesses, but no related series.	33	36	31
Multiple injuries and/or illnesses, with at least one related series.	19	25	40
Total:	**100**	**100**	**100**

In general, then, we developed summaries and indexes in the major areas of interview response: physical, emotional, injury or illness incidence, and socializing. We selected those specific questions which most discriminated between Labor Performance Summary Groups. These latter groups themselves had been derived from a number of questionnaire items which we felt were highly indicative of work adjustment

16

following the most serious compensated injury since the start of 1950. We were then able to cross-tabulate the Labor Performance Summary Groups, representing our central concern, or major dependent variable in our study, with the various other summaries and indexes, and the numerous other items on our questionnaire which are not parts of any of these summary groups or indexes.

[2]

Summary and Implications

What happens to men who become seriously and permanently disabled insofar as their subsequent employment is concerned? There has been considerable speculation, but few facts exist to answer this question. This study, therefore, examined the work experiences of a number of such men to determine empirically just what does happen to them. Since men who have been seriously and permanently injured on the job can be identified relatively easily through workmen's compensation boards, this study was limited to a group of such men, and did not attempt to obtain a cross section of all men who are seriously and permanently disabled. We believe that the work experiences of on-the-job accident victims should be representative of all disabled men,[1] other than those with congenital disabilities or perhaps those who were injured in war.

Accordingly, a cross section of men injured on the job in the New York Metropolitan Area, during the early and middle 1950s, was obtained from the three agencies which have jurisdiction there: the United States Bureau of Employees' Compensation, the New Jersey Division of Workmen's Compensation, and the New York Workmen's Compensation

---

[1] Findings of the study strongly support this initial hypothesis. Almost two-thirds of the men in the sample had experienced serious injuries or illnesses more than once in their adult lives, and these additional episodes were a "mix" of the on-the-job and off-the-job occurrences. Strictly occupational diseases were rare, and injuries or illnesses at work or elsewhere were similar both in kind and in agency, arguing similar effects on employment. Only compensation itself appears to differentiate on- and off-the-job accidents.

19

Board. About 1300 of these men were then interviewed to ascertain their employment histories or current (1960) labor force status.[2]

In the United States (in 1959-60) it is estimated that there were some 3,300,000 men between the ages of 17 and 64 with major activity limitations—i.e., serious, and permanent disabilities—who were working at the time the limitation started. There were also another 2,200,000 aged 65 and over whose limitation started while working. The number of 3,300,-000 shows how great has been the impact of these injuries upon men of working age throughout this country (Appendix B). Our study, in essence, reports the experiences of such men in the New York Metropolitan Area labor market.

SUMMARY OF MAJOR FINDINGS

1) Prior to the injury which brought the men into our study, their employment histories seem to have been generally similar to those of all men in the New York Metropolitan Area. However, men who became injured on the job were much more likely to have been manual workers rather than white-collar workers, and to have worked in construction and manufacturing rather than in offices or stores.

At the time of injury these men had earned median weekly wages of some $90—about the same as for the New York area in 1955 (the approximate average date of injury). Further, in the three years prior to their injury they had consistently worked; fewer than 1 man in 4 had suffered more than one month of unemployment in these three years. Clearly, the available evidence does not indicate that they were marginal workers prior to their injury on the job. Nor do we have any evidence that these men were "accident prone," if there be such a phenomenon. In short, they seem to have been an ordinary cross section of manual workers.

2) Fourteen per cent of the disabled men were not employed at the time of interview (1960). This includes those seeking work as well as those who left the labor force, for we cannot distinguish between these two groups. This non-employment rate seems to be a little less than double that of the male population in the New York Metropolitan Area in 1960. The greater incidence of non-employment is particularly pro-

---

[2] See Appendix A for a detailed description of the population studied. See especially Table A.1.

nounced among men aged 45 and over; 17 per cent of these older men were not employed, as compared with 11 per cent of men under age 45. Of the disabled men who had worked during the year preceding the interview, about one-fifth had worked part time and four-fifths full time. Among all men in the New York Metropolitan Area, a smaller proportion had worked part time during the year. Again the differences were most pronounced for men aged 45 and over. Among these older men 24 per cent of the disabled had worked part time, in comparison with 14 per cent among the younger disabled workers.

3) In addition to ascertaining employment in terms of being employed full time, part time, or not employed, we also ascertained it in terms of the quality of the job (if any) held in the year preceding the interview. The men were divided into three groups: a) those who had worked at full-time jobs in the year preceding the interview, and had earned higher wages than at the time of their injury, b) those who had worked full time but at the same or lower wages than at the time of injury, and c) those who had worked only part time or not at all, or had earned very little in the year preceding the interview. Let us call the third group the employment "failures."

Who are these "failures?" In general, they resemble the unemployed men in the whole United States. They tend to be the older, less well educated, semi-skilled or unskilled, Negro or Puerto Rican. In addition, many of them are men who have had more than one injury—often chain injuries, i.e., recurrences of previous injuries—and many have emotional problems in addition to health problems. The outstanding observation is that these "failures" resemble the unemployed in general, only more so, and, in addition, have physical problems which diminish further their employment prospects.

On the other hand, the disabled men who were successfully employed (group *a* above) tend to resemble the successfully employed in the general male population—the younger, better educated, skilled or white-collar workers (Chapter 5).

4) Lest the preceding comments give the impression that disability *per se* is irrelevant, we wish to emphasize here that it is indeed relevant. First, about 1 man in 20 never returned to work because of the severity of his injury. For those who did return to work, the disability seems to have compounded their job-seeking problems. In particular, if the man

21

had several injuries, he was much more likely not to be employed, or to have worked only part time or at very poor paying jobs. On the other hand, the particular part of the body injured does not seem in itself to be especially important so far as employment is concerned.

Disability seems to have compounded the older man's job problem even more than the younger man's. We cannot say from our data, however, whether this resulted solely from the fact that, as a consequence of the disabling accident, he lost his job and had to seek a new one, or whether his more difficult employment problems resulted solely from the physical or emotional effects of the injury. The evidence suggests a mixture of all these factors.

Adjustment to the labor market was also related to the year of most recent injury. Those injured in 1957 or later (regardless of whether this was the injury that put them into our study) were more likely to be "failures,"—i.e., to have worked only part time or not at all. There was, however, no significant difference between those injured in 1955-56 and those injured earlier. This finding suggests that it may take several years—perhaps as many as three or four—before a large number of the disabled recover sufficiently to re-enter the labor market at a level of employment equal to the best they are likely to get. After that initial period of three to four years, however, length of time in the labor market seems to make little difference so far as employment is concerned.

5) The character of the first job obtained by the injured worker upon re-entry into the labor force was an excellent indicator of future labor market activities—at least for the next five years or so (i.e., up to the time of the interview). If the disabled worker returned to work for the same firm for which he had worked at the time of injury and to the same occupation, he was most likely to have a good job five years later. On the other hand, if he found employment with a different firm, or changed occupation, he was more likely to have a poor job—or no job—five years later.

Generally, returning to work for the same firm meant returning to the same occupation. About two men in three returned to the same firm, and of these about 80 per cent returned also to the same occupation. Of the remaining one-third of the men who did not return to work for the same firm, only about one-quarter were able to find employment in the same occupation. Men who had changed both firm and occupation were generally found to be job "failures" five years later.

22

Those who returned to the same firm tended to get back to work sooner, and at the same, or higher, wage rate. Only 9 per cent of them went back at a wage rate lower than that at the time of injury, whereas a total of 54 per cent of those who did not return to the same firm went back at a lower rate. This is an important difference, for in both groups the pattern of higher or lower wages, once established, tended to maintain itself. When interviewed, half of those who had returned to the same firm following the accident, had worked full time (during the year preceding the interview) and in a better paying job than at the time of injury. Only a third of those who had not returned had worked full time at better pay. Of the first group, 12 per cent had a much worse job or none at all; in the second group this figure rose to one-third. Finally, those whose first job after injury was with the former firm had steadier work during the three years preceding the interview (Chapter 6).

6) Other information concerning a disabled man at the time of injury can indicate whether he may become a job "failure." He may be: victim of a chain injury (i.e., recurrence of an earlier injury); older; poorly educated; a semi-skilled or unskilled worker at the time of his injury; Negro or Puerto Rican.

We may apply these criteria as follows: a) select out all men with chain injuries; b) of the remainder, select out those who did not return to work for the same firm; c) of the remainder, select out those aged 45 and over and who had only eight years or less of schooling. If such screening procedures are applied to the entire population of disabled men, we shall have screened out about half of them. Among this half will be some four-fifths of all the future job "failures" plus perhaps two-thirds of those who will make only partially successful job adjustments. These "failures" and "partial successes" are the ones who need rehabilitation services—medical, social, psychiatric, and vocational (Chapter 7).

7) Relatively few men—about 1 in 10—received any vocational training following their injury. Since about 6 out of 10 men returned to work for the same firm and in the same occupation, presumably they did not need retraining. Presumably also, at least some of the remaining 4 men in 10 could have used retraining; we have no way of knowing whether they would have accepted and used it (Chapter 8).

These, then, are some highlights of the findings from this study. Together with numerous other materials discussed in the succeeding chap-

23

ters, they suggest that, apart from the relatively few cases of extreme handicap (men confined to beds or wheelchairs, sufferers from major brain damage), the problem of the male worker who has been seriously and permanently disabled on the job is, in many ways, a part of the more general problem of unemployment. In many instances, the disability itself seems to be of secondary importance to subsequent experience in the labor market when viewed alongside the relevance of such old and familiar factors as race and ethnic group, age, years of schooling, and skill. Its major importance, in the majority of cases, seems to derive less from what it does to the individual as a person than from the fact that it makes a worker unemployed. Disablement forces him to seek work, possibly deprives him of seniority rights, and, most important of all, subjects him once again to the mesh of impersonal categorizations by which firms select their employees: age, ethnic group, schooling, etc. And in the process of such job seeking, his disability emerges as an extra liability, in addition to older age or ethnic origin or lack of schooling.

SOME IMPLICATIONS

1) Ultimately the majority of disabled workers apparently obtain employment without assistance from any special agencies. Indeed, some 4 men in 10 ultimately have better jobs than the ones they held at the time of their injury; another 4 in 10 have jobs which, compared with the job at the time of injury, are about the same or somewhat poorer. These men seem to have made their job adjustments largely on their own. Either the disabled man's original firm rehired him, or he went out and found a new job for himself. Neither the public employment agencies nor the rehabilitation agencies seem to have played an important role.

The remaining men, however,—the 2 men in 10—clearly need considerable rehabilitation if even a portion of them are to become reasonably satisfactorily employed. Not only do they need vocational aid; apparently they also need additional medical and psychiatric treatment. Furthermore, they tend to be the types of men who, even when not disabled, have difficulty in finding jobs. In short, these are the difficult cases. Yet, except for medical treatment, these men seem not to have received any other rehabilitation. We have no way of knowing how many would accept and complete rehabilitation programs, and become employed and self-supporting. But clearly these are the men who need the maximum rehabilitation efforts, and have not received such aid.

24

2) Now it would seem that there are more than enough cases of seriously and permanently disabled men of working age (17 to 64 years), who are not usually working, to fill the available rehabilitation facilities. There are about one and one-half million such men in the United States. In comparison, only some 200,000 cases are handled by the state rehabilitation agencies each year; these include women, youngsters and "senior" citizens as well as men of working age. Furthermore, each year there seem to be about 700,000 new cases of men between the ages of 17 and 64 who become victims of a chronic activity limitation which can lead to their becoming not employed.

In short, rehabilitation facilities need considerable expansion, and the agencies should make increased efforts to rehabilitate those most in need of such services.

3) Since the disabled man's future employment status is so closely dependent upon whether or not he returns to work for his original firm, further study of why some return and others do not is needed. Our study was unable to obtain sufficient information on this point; a new study would need to be quite differently designed.

4) Additional studies along the lines of ours, but for different labor markets, should be carried out in an effort to determine how applicable our findings may be to the entire United States.

5) The workmens' compensation, rehabilitation, and employment systems should work even more closely together than they now do. If properly coordinated, the former can, almost at the time of accident, pick out the men most likely to need rehabilitation efforts. Rehabiliation and job placement efforts can then be undertaken immediately.

Part I

EMPLOYMENT STATUS OF THE DISABLED MEN

[3]

Employment Experience in 1959-1960

The employment situation of the men in our study was measured in several ways, on the basis of diverse information collected during the course of the interviews, the great majority of which were conducted during 1960. In this chapter we are reporting on two such measures: a) whether the man did, or did not, have a job at the time of the interview; and b) whether he worked at all during the year preceding the interview, and, if so, for how long. In addition, we are presenting the occupational distribution of those who were working at the time of interview.

The great majority of the men employed at the time of the interview had, of course, worked during much or all of the preceding year. So also had some who were not employed at the time of the interview. Let us now examine each of these two groups separately.

EMPLOYMENT SITUATION AT TIME OF INTERVIEW

Most of the men whom we studied were employed at the time of the interview. But most adult men in the United States are ordinarily employed. The significant question is whether there was any difference beween the proportions employed among the men whom we studied and

29

among the general male population—a difference which might conceivably have something to do with the fact that the men in our study were permanently disabled.

Eighty-six per cent of the men studied were employed at the time of the interview; and 14 per cent were not employed, a figure which includes those seeking work as well as those who had left the labor force.[1] This proportion not employed is substantially higher than that for all men in the New York Metropolitan Area, among whom 92 per cent were employed and 8 per cent were not employed.[2] Thus the proportion not employed among the group of permanently disabled workers was significantly greater than among all workers.

The proportions not employed among all men in the New York Metropolitan Area, and among the disabled whom we studied, were as follows:

Age	All men	Disabled men
25 to 34 years	9%	11%
35 to 44 years	7	11
45 to 54 years	9	17

Whether 14 per cent not employed is considered to be "large" or "small" depends on how one approaches the problem. Certainly, if only 8 per cent of the disabled had turned out to be not employed, we should have concluded that this group did not differ from the general population of comparable workers. On the other hand, if the reader takes seriously some of the speeches which have been delivered from time to time, one might expect to find perhaps only half of the disabled men at work. Obviously, then, the men whom we studied had less employment than did men of the same age distribution in the general population, but certainly not as little as some of the popular literature would suggest.

The fact that the rate of non-employment among the disabled increases

---

[1] Interestingly, virtually identical estimates were obtained from a cross section sample of the disabled population in the entire United States population, surveyed in March and April, 1960, by the Survey Research Center. Of all disabled men aged 35 to 54 (the approximate age range of the men whom we studied) 85 per cent were employed and 15 per cent were not employed. See *The Economic Position of Disabled Workers, and Their Future Prospects* by Martin David, James Morgan, Wilbur Cohen, Harvey Brazer, Ann Arbor, Survey Research Center, Institute for Social Research, University of Michigan, November, 1961, p. 30.

[2] U. S. Census of Population, 1960, *op. cit.*, Table 115. Percentages refer to men between the ages of 25 and 54 years.

30

very sharply with increasing age is highly significant. At each of the three ages the rate is higher among the disabled men than among the general male population. Yet at ages 25 to 34 years the rate among the disabled was only one-fourth higher than that in the male population of the entire Metropolitan Area. However, among the men aged 45 to 54 years, there were twice as many not employed among the disabled as among the general population.

That the employment problems of the older disabled man become interwoven with the problems of older workers in general can be seen more clearly by examining the rates of non-employment among the disabled men we interviewed, in detailed age groups as follows (see also Chart 3-1):

	Per cent		
Age	*Employed*	*Not employed*	*Total*
25 to 34 years	89%	11%	100%
35 to 39 years	93	7	100
40 to 44 years	86	14	100
45 to 49 years	88	12	100
50 to 54 years	79	21	100

By age 50 to 54, about 1 disabled man in 5 is not employed. Among the total male population of the Metropolitan Area this rate is not reached until 60 to 64, an age at which 22 per cent were not employed in 1960. The significance of this difference for purposes of rehabilitation and employment is discussed in detail in Chapter 7.

AMOUNT OF EMPLOYMENT DURING THE YEAR
PRECEDING THE INTERVIEW

Just as the disabled whom we studied had a somewhat smaller proportion employed at the time of the interview, compared with the proportion in the general population, so we find also that a somewhat smaller proportion of the disabled were fully employed during the preceding year. For purposes of this analysis *full time* work is defined as working 35 hours or more per week, and in 40 or more weeks during the preceding year. All other men who worked any amount of time during the preceding year were classified as having worked *part time.*

The proportions of full-time versus part-time workers among the disabled cannot be compared exactly with the total Metropolitan Area male population, since for the latter we have information only on number of weeks worked in 1959. The rates by age for the two groups are as follows:

Disabled Workers in the Labor Market

	Disabled men			All men in New York Metropolitan Area 1959a		
Worked	Under Age 45	Age 45+	Total	Under Age 45	Age 45+	Total
Full time	86%	76%	81%	91%	91%	91%
Part time	14	24	19	9	9	9
Total	100%	100%	100%	100%	100%	100%

a Ages 25 to 44 years, and 45 to 54 years. Full time is defined as having worked any number of hours in 40 or more weeks. (From U.S. Census of Population, 1960, *op. cit.*, Table 118.)

Most significantly, the differences among men under 45 years of age are much smaller than among the older men. Clearly the older disabled men have a much less favorable employment situation as compared with the younger men.

Chart 3-1. PER CENT OF DISABLED MEN WHO WERE NOT EMPLOYED IN 1960, ACCORDING TO AGE OF MEN

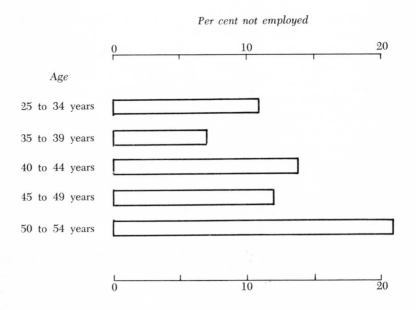

32

OCCUPATIONS OF THE EMPLOYED

The large majority of the disabled men were manual workers. Over half were in the groups "craftsmen, foremen, or kindred workers" and "operatives and kindred workers." Very few were in the professional or managerial occupations. That the occupational distribution of the disabled differed markedly from that of all men (aged 20 to 59) in the New York Metropolitan Area in 1960[3] is seen as follows:

Occupation	*All men*	*Disabled men*
Professional, technical, kindred workers	15%	4%
Managers, officials, proprietors, excl. farm	15	10
Clerical and sales workers	20	13
Total white-collar workers	**50**	**27**
Craftsmen, foremen, kindred workers	21	31
Operatives and kindred workers	14	23
Service workers	10	10
Laborers	5	9
Total manual workers	**50**	**73**
All workers	**100%**	**100%**

The occupational distribution of the disabled men reflects in part the hazards of the industries in which they worked, both at the time of interview and the time of the disabling injury,[4] and in part the fact that these men were in general less well educated than the male population of the New York Metropolitan Area. The median number of years of schooling completed among the disabled men was 10.4, as compared with 12.1 years for all men in the Metropolitan Area. Most importantly, because they were employed in these manual occupations, they were more subject to the risk of unemployment (see Chapter 4) than is the general male population of the area.

SUMMARY

When compared with the general male population in the New York Metropolitan Area, the employment rates for the younger disabled men (those under 45 years of age) were somewhat lower. But the younger disabled men, in comparison with the disabled aged 45 and over, were

---

[3] U. S. Census of Population, 1960, *op. cit.*, Table 123.

[4] See Chapter 6 for further discussion of changes in occupations between time of injury and time of interview.

Disabled Workers in the Labor Market

more likely to be employed at the time of interview, and were also more likely to have been fully employed during the preceding year, than were the older disabled men.

Among disabled men aged 45 and over, the employment situation was very noticeably worse than among the general male population of comparable age. Apparently, the employment problems faced by the "older worker"[5] are compounded when he is also disabled. But we cannot say whether this results from loss of his job due to the disabling accident and subsequent necessity of seeking a new job, or whether his more difficult employment problems result from the injury's having a worse physical or emotional effect upon him—or both of these.

Finally, we noted that the disabled men were occupied in precisely those job categories where the risks of unemployment are highest, namely, in manual jobs.

---

[5] See for example, Clark Tibbitts and Wilma Donahue, editors, *Social and Psychological Aspects of Aging*, New York, Columbia University Press, 1962; various articles in the section *Factors Affecting Work and Retirement*. See especially, Walt R. Simmons, "The Matrix of Health, Manpower, and Age" (pp. 208-17), and A. J. Jaffe and J. R. Milavsky, "Unemployment, Retirement, and Pensions" (pp. 279-92).

34

[4]

Characteristics of Disabled Men
Who Were Not Employed

We have already seen that some 14 per cent of the disabled men in our study were not employed at the time of interview (1960). Small as it may seem, this proportion is still almost twice that in the comparable age groups for all men in the New York Metropolitan Area. Therefore, let us now examine the characteristics of these men; a knowledge of them should be useful for purposes of vocational rehabilitation and reemployment.

COMPARISON OF THE DISABLED MEN WITH THE AMERICAN MALE POPULATION, 1960[1]

The disabled men who were not employed at the time of interview tended to resemble those not employed in the general male population of the United States. They tended to be older, either not married or separated from their wives, less well educated, Negro or Puerto Rican,[2] not

---

[1] Comparative data for the New York Metropolitan Area were not as yet available at the time this manuscript was prepared.

[2] There is a high relationship between level of education and ethnic stock among the disabled men as well as in the general population. The distribution of the men in our study was as follows:

	Educational level			
	8th grade or less	grades 9 through 11	12+ grades	Total
White (excl. Puerto Rican)	33%	31%	36%	100%
Negro and Puerto Rican	58	23	19	100%

35

Disabled Workers in the Labor Market

war veterans, and in less skilled manual occcupations. Approximate comparisons of the disabled whom we studied and the male population of the United States are as follows:[3]

1) The percentages not employed increase with age:

	25 to 44	45 to 54
Disabled men	11%	17%
All men in United States	6	8

2) The percentages not employed were lower among war veterans:

	Veteran	Non-veteran
Disabled men	11%	20%
All men in United States	6	7

3) The percentages not employed decrease by level of schooling:

	Under 9 grades	9-12 grades	Some college
Disabled men	22%	12%	5%
All men in U.S.[a] (ages 30-54)	12	7	5

[a] Computed from data in United States Bureau of the Census, *U. S. Census of Population: 1950*, V. IV, *Special Reports,* Part 5, Chapter B, Education, Washington, U. S. Government Printing Office, 1953, Table 9.

4) Married men living with their wives were less likely to be unemployed:

	Married and living with wife	All others
Disabled men	13%	30%
All men in United States	4	8

5) We find similar patterns of non-employment by major occupational groups, as seen in the following indexes (the non-employment rate for service workers and laborers equals 100):

	White-collar occupations	Craftsmen & kindred	Operatives	Service workers & laborers
Disabled men	43	52	71	100
All men in U.S.	22	56	67	100

[3] Data for the male population of the United States derived from Robert L. Stein and Herman Travis, *Labor Force and Employment in 1960*, Special Labor Force Report No. 14, U. S. Bureau of Labor Statistics, Reprint No. 2365, April 1961; and Arnold Katz, *Educational Attainment of Workers*, 1959, Special Labor Force Report No. 1, U. S. Bureau of Labor Statistics, Reprint No. 333, Feb. 1960. Wherever feasible, we have compared characteristics by age group for males in the total United States to correspond as closely as possible with the age groups of the disabled men we studied.

36

Characteristics of Disabled Men Who Were Not Employed

6) Among the white (excluding Puerto Rican) disabled men, 13 per cent were not employed as compared with 30 per cent of all other men. Among the male population of the U.S., 4 per cent of the whites in the labor force (i.e., those gainfully employed or looking for work) were unemployed, as compared with 9 per cent of the non-whites (See also Chart 4-1).

Although the rates of non-employment among the disabled whom we studied are not directly comparable in all respects to those of the male population of the United States, they clearly reveal the same patterns. The highest rates of non-employment among the disabled whom we interviewed were found in those very groups with the highest rates in the total population.

THE PHYSICAL AND EMOTIONAL CONDITIONS OF THE DISABLED MEN

Among the men whom we interviewed those who were not employed were more likely than the ones employed to have physical or emotional problems (or both); they were more likely to claim some kind of limitation on either their work or non-work activities; and they were more likely to have had a chain injury—i.e., an injury with one or more recurrences, each of which added a definite increment to the original disability. Although information about the prevalence of these characteristics among the total male population of the United Sates is largely unavailable, we suspect that this pattern among the disabled is closely similar to the pattern among all non-employed men in this country. The distribution by employment status among the disabled men we studied was as follows:

Self-evaluation	Employed	Not employed
Mentioned having:	54%	87%
Both physical and emotional problems	17	58
Physical problems only	14	16
Emotional problems only	23	13
No mention:	46	13
Total:	**100%**	**100%**

Physical limitation	Employed	Not employed
Claimed some physical limitation	72%	92%
Claimed no physical limitation	28	8
Total:	**100%**	**100%**

Chain injury	Employed	Not employed
Reported such a series	22%	41%
Did not report such a series	78	59
Total:	**100%**	**100%**

37

Chart 4-1. PER CENT OF DISABLED MEN WHO WERE NOT EMPLOYED IN 1960, ACCORDING TO THE PERSONAL CHARACTERISTICS OF THE MEN

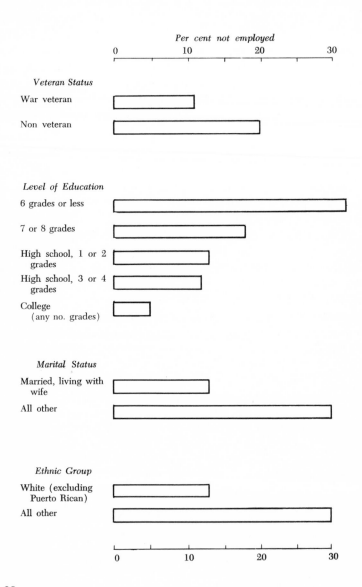

38

There is good reason to believe that the physical condition of the men whom we studied is fairly objectively reported (within interview limits, and considering the fact that no medical examinations were carried out as part of this study). This is so because of several considerations. a) The men studied had been declared to have permanent disabilities by the workmen's compensation boards. b) In classifying a man as having a physical problem one criterion used was whether the interviewer reported that the handicap was visible; if it was visible to the interviewer it would be visible to an employer whose judgment, and subsequent hiring practice, might be affected by what he saw. c) A cluster of injuries or illnesses in the period between the time of injury and the time of interview served to put the man in our classification of "physical problem"; in many cases these men had chain injuries, e.g., a series of recurrent "back troubles."[4]

With regard to mentions of "emotional problems," presumably such responses are more subjective than those for "physical problems." Nevertheless, emotional and psychological problems (whatever their origin) are often deterrents to accomplishments, as well as sometimes being "rationalizations" for failure in the labor market.

FAMILY INCOME

Total family income (in the year preceding the interview) was significantly lower among the families of the men who were not employed. The respective medians were: $4400 for the families of men who were not employed; $6800 for the families of men who were employed. In general, the disabled who were not employed tended to resemble the low-income people and families of New York, as these have been so well described by John G. Myers in *Income Distribution and Economic Welfare in New York State.*[5]

NUMBER OF YEARS SINCE INJURY

The number of years between the time of injury (i.e., the injury which brought the man into our study) and the time of interview was unrelated to the employment status of the younger men. However, among men

---

[4] See also Chapter 1, section on "Summary Groups and Indexes."

[5] State of New York, Department of Labor, Division of Research and Statistics, Special Bulletin No. 236, March 1961.

aged 45 and over, the percentage not employed was significantly higher for those who had been more recently injured. The percentages not employed are as follows:

Year of injury	Under age 45	Age 45+
1950 through 1954	11%	14%
1955 to September 1957[a]	11	20

[a] No men were interviewed whose workmen's compensation accident occurred after September 1957.

In short, it seems either that the older worker is more adversely affected in a physical sense by his injury (although we have no evidence on this point); or, regardless of the degree of disability, it takes him longer to recover; or it is harder for him to regain his employed status once he leaves it. That unemployment generally weighs more heavily on the older worker[6] certainly suggests the likelihood of the last possibility. But it is probable that all three are relevant to some extent.

INDUSTRY OF EMPLOYMENT AT TIME OF INJURY

In each industrial classification, the older worker was less likely than the younger worker to be employed. There were substantial age differences among the various industrial groupings, however. The differences by age were greatest in transportation and communication, where the proportion not employed was more than two and a half times as high among older workers as among younger workers, and in construction, where it was nearly twice as high. The differences were least in the service industries, where the proportion not employed among the older workers was only 13 per cent higher than among the younger, and in finance and public administration, where it was only a third higher.

---

[6] See for example, A. J. Jaffe, Jeanne B. Anderson, Mabel Hopper, D. Staffler, and J. R. Milavsky, *Unemployment Benefits and Family Finances . . .* A Study of Income and Expenditures of Beneficiaries and Their Families in Utica, New York, 1958, Albany, N. Y. State Department of Labor, Division of Employment, Bureau of Research and Statistics, February, 1960. See also Clark Tibbitts, Arthur J. Noetzel, Jr., and Charles C. Gibbons, *Employment of the Older Worker: Two Papers and a Bibliography,* Kalamazoo, Mich., The W. E. Upjohn Institute For Employment Research, Sept., 1959. See also Clark Tibbitts and Wilma Donahue, editors, *Social and Psychological Aspects of Aging, op. cit.*

Characteristics of Disabled Men Who Were Not Employed

The percentages of men not employed by industry and age are as follows:

Industry group	Under age 45	Age 45+
Construction and mining	9%	17%
Manufacturing	10	15
Transportation, communication, and public utilities	7	19
Trade	10	16
Services	15	17
Finance and public administration	19	25

PART OF BODY INJURED

When subdivided into broad location of injury categories, we find but little difference in the proportions not employed. The rate of non-employment was highest among those with head injuries and lowest among those with injuries to the upper extermities. But the differences, especially between upper and lower extremities, trunk, and "other," were not very great. (Chart 4-2).

Division into our two age groupings enlarges some of these differences, however. Head injuries among older workers become the ones most prominently associated with not being employed. But the effect of age is particularly pronounced among those with lower extremity and "other" injuries (i.e., internal injuries, occupational diseases, injuries to more than one part of the body). The proportion not employed among men with these disabilities was about two and a half times as high among the older men as among the younger. But among those with head or trunk injuries, non-employment among the older men was only half again as high as among the younger; and among those with injuries to the upper extremities there was really no difference between the non-employment rates of older and younger men. (Chart 4-2).

EMPLOYMENT PRIOR TO ACCIDENT

During the three years preceding the injury that brought them into our study, the large majority of the men interviewed had been out of work for less than one month. Accordingly, we may ask: is there any relationship between length of time out of work in the three years preceding the accident and the employment status in 1960 (when we interviewed)?

41

Disabled Workers in the Labor Market

The non-employment rates in 1960, by age in that year and by number of months not employed in the three years preceding injury, were as follows:

Months not employed during three years preceding disablement	Per cent not employed Under age 45	Age 45+
Less than one month	6%	21%
One month or longer	17	20

A younger man—one under age 40 or 45—who worked consistently and missed less than one month of work in the three years preceding his accident, was quite likely to be employed some five years later. In fact, the likelihood of being employed was about the same as that for all men—disabled or not.

However, the younger man who had been out of work for more than a month (in the three years preceding his accident), or the older man—regardless of his previous employment—had only 4 chances in 5 of being employed some five years later. Thus, increasing age equalized employment opportunities between workers with different employment histories prior to injury, primarily by increasing the non-employment rate among older men with better work histories.

SUMMARY

(1) The employment status of the men in our study was probably affected by much the same kinds of conditions and attributes as affect the employment status of all men in the society. Puerto Ricans and non-whites, those with less formal schooling, and those who worked at semi-skilled or unskilled and lower paying occupations, were less likely to be employed than were those in the more favored classifications.

(2) Not surprisingly, non-employment was more likely among those who mentioned having some kind of physical or emotional problem, though it was impossible to determine to what extent these were excuses by those who had, in a sense, "failed," or whether they were actually valid statements of fact. Of importance in this connection is the fact that even among those with the most such mentions, the proportion not employed never reached a half; and altogether, despite our attempts to exclude all but the seriously and permanently disabled, the non-employment rate among the disabled men in our sample amounted to only 14 per cent. In short, many men who mentioned having physical or emotional problems nevertheless were employed.

42

Chart 4-2. PER CENT OF DISABLED MEN WHO WERE NOT EMPLOYED IN 1960, ACCORDING TO PART OF BODY INJURED AND ACCORDING TO AGE

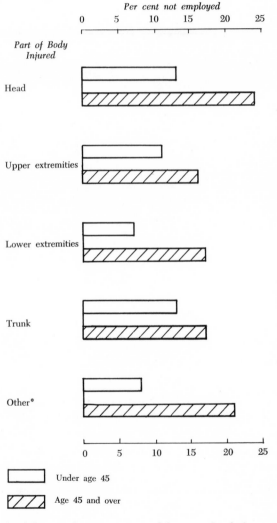

* Includes internal injuries, occupational diseases, and multiple injuries.

43

[5]

Quality of Jobs Held by the Disabled Worker

Obtaining a job is but one indication of readjustment to the labor market. The great majority of the men studied—86 per cent—were employed some five years after their disabling accident, and might for that reason be said to have made a "successful" adjustment. But simply being employed is not a sufficient criterion of "successful" or "unsuccessful" adjustment. It is just as important to know whether the disabled man regained at least his former wage level, and whether he found employment at a level of skill and continuity of work that compares reasonably favorably with what he had before becoming disabled.

Accordingly, in this chapter we shall divide our respondents into three groups on the basis of the quality of their employment during the 12 months preceding the interview. To assess quality of employment we shall use three criteria:[1] (1) weekly wages at time of interview as compared with weekly wages at time of injury, (2) number of hours worked per week, and (3) number of weeks worked per year (in the year preceding the interview). Those assumed to have a "better" job (i.e., the ones we assigned to the top category) were men who had worked full time during the previous twelve months (i.e., at least 35 hours a week for at least 40 weeks of the year) and who at the same time received wages at least $10 a week more than at the time they became disabled.[2]

---

[1] See also Chapter 1, section on "Summary Groups and Indexes."

[2] The large majority of these full-time workers—75 per cent—reported weekly earnings greater by $20 or more than at the time of their injury.

45

Disabled Workers in the Labor Market

Those assigned to the second category, "same or somewhat poorer" jobs, were men who worked full time during the preceding year, but at a weekly wage less than $10 above what they were earning at the time of their accident. Included in this group were men who were earning less than at the time of injury.[3] Those put in the third category, "very poor or no" jobs, either did not work during the 12 months preceding the interview, or worked only part time at a loss in wages.

The criteria for full-time employment need no explanation. But the reason for choosing the figure of a $10 increase in weekly wages as the criterion for improved position may appear a bit obscure. This figure is a conservative estimate of the increase a male worker in the New York Metropolitan Area would have had to receive in order to keep up with wage changes during the approximate period between injury and interview.[4] Anything less than this represents a relative, and in some cases an actual, decline. Because this is a *conservative* estimate, however, it is probable that our category of "better" contains some who in actuality did not better their positions, vis-á-vis others in their occupational categories.

Application of these criteria provides the following distribution of the disabled workers some five years after their accident:

> 41 per cent were in "better" jobs
> 39 per cent were in "same or somewhat poorer" jobs
> 20 per cent had "very poor or no" jobs

SOME CHARACTERISTICS OF THEIR PRESENT JOBS

Class of Worker. Only 10 per cent of the workers were self-employed at the time of interview. By definition, their self-employment represented

---

[3] Of these men, 54 per cent reported slight increases in weekly earnings; 22 per cent reported wage losses of $20 or more.

[4] Average weekly or hourly earnings increased between 20 and 25 per cent between 1955 (the average year of accident for the men whom we studied) and 1960 (the year of interview) for skilled maintenance workers and unskilled plant workers in New York City, Newark, and Jersey City. (See "Job Pay Levels and Trends in 60 Labor Markets," in *Monthly Labor Review*, pp. 163 to 176, United States Dept. of Labor, Bureau of Labor Statistics, February, 1961, V. 84, No. 2). Also, in New York City average weekly earnings in durable manufacturing increased by 18 per cent between 1955 and 1960, by 19 per cent in non-durable manufacturing, and by 32 per cent in construction. (See appropriate monthly issues of *Labor Market Review*, published by New York State Department of Labor.) Since the median weekly earnings of these men was about $92 at the time of their accident, we could have used a minimum increase of $18 weekly as the criterion for inclusion in the top, or "better" job, category. See also fn. 2, this chapter.

46

a change in class of worker status, since all were employees at time of injury. Judging from their weekly earnings (at the time of interview) these men did somewhat less well than did those men employed in "better" jobs,—median earnings of $100 weekly as compared with $118; on the other hand, the self-employed earned somewhat more than did those men in the "same or somewhat poorer" job category, who averaged $93.

Weekly Earnings. As could be expected, those who experienced an improvement in their jobs between the time of injury and time of interview were generally earning more at the latter date than were those who were in the "same or somewhat poorer" job category. The average (median) weekly wages at the time of injury and at the time of interview for the two groups were as follows:

		At time of interview, those in . . .	
Weekly earnings (median)	*"Better" jobs*	*"Same or poorer" jobs*	*"Very poor or no" jobs*a
At time of injury	$88	$99	$86
At time of interview	$118	$93	$77
Change:	Increase $30	Decrease $6	Decrease $9

a Includes only those who had earnings at any time within 12 months preceding interview.

There was considerable overlap in earnings, however. Of those in the "better" jobs, about 1 man in 4 had weekly earnings of less than $90 at the time of interview; on the other hand, of those men in "same or somewhat poorer" jobs, 1 man in 5 was earning $125 or more per week. Still, the dominant relationships were in the expected directions: the majority of the men in the lowest weekly-earnings brackets (at the time of interview) had suffered losses in earnings, while the majority of those in the highest weekly-earnings brackets had experienced gains. The percentage distribution of labor performance groups by wage changes follows:

	Increase			*Total % with in-*	*Decrease*		*Total % with de-*
Labor performance group	*$20+*	*$10-19*	*$0-9*	*crease*	*$0-19*	*$20+*	*crease*
"Better" jobs	75%	25%	0%	100	0%	0%	0
"Same or poorer" jobs	2a	1a	54	57	22	21	43
"Very poor or no" jobs*	3a	3a	36	42	22	36	58

* Persons with no jobs are counted as having experienced a decrease of $20 or more.

a When interviewed, these men were receiving higher weekly wages than at the

47

Disabled Workers in the Labor Market

FAMILY AND PERSONAL CHARACTERISTICS

Family Income. During the year preceding the interview, the median family income of the men in the "better" jobs was about $7,400. This amount included the wages and earnings of the disabled man, the earnings of any other members of the household who were employed, any social insurance payments received (such as workmen's compensation or pensions), any income obtained from rent or property or from self-employment, etc.

The families of men in the "same or somewhat poorer" job category had a median income of $6,200.

In the New York Metropolitan Area median family income was $6,800 in 1959.[5] Evidently the families of men with "better" jobs were a little more prosperous than families in the entire area, and those of men in the "same or somewhat poorer" jobs were less prosperous.

Poorest of all were the families of men in the "very poor or no" job category where median income was about $4,550. This amount is somewhat above that of all families in the Metropolitan Area in which the head did not work during 1959, or worked less than 13 weeks; among such families median income was about $3,000. Despite this comparison, $4,550 is a low median and means that half the families had incomes below this amount. Precisely where the "poverty" line should be drawn we cannot say, but that many of these families may have been hardship cases seems highly probable.

There was considerable variation in family income. At the poorest extreme it was found that 8 per cent of the families had annual incomes of under $3,000, whereas at the wealthiest extreme, 13 per cent had incomes of $10,000 and over. The distribution of family income for all disabled men was as follows:

---

time of injury, but were working only on a part-time basis. Individual analysis of their interview schedules, with respect to other labor force variables, showed them to have done less well than those assigned to the "better" job category, e.g., a construction worker who received a high weekly wage but had worked only three weeks during the year preceding the interview.

[5] Family income classified by occupation of head was weighted in accordance with the distribution of occupations among the men we studied. This provided the most nearly comparable family income data for the New York Metropolitan Area that we could obtain. Data on 1959 family income from U. S. Census of Population, 1960, *op. cit.*, Table 145.

48

Income class	Per cent
Under $3,000	8
$3,000 to $3,999	9
$4,000 to $4,999	12
$5,000 to $5,999	17
$6,000 to $6,999	13
$7,000 to $9,999	28
$10,000 and over	13
Total	**100%**

Size of Family. The only significant difference in family size associated with better employment for the disabled man was the greater likelihood that a one-person family (i.e., one in which the disabled man lived alone) would be in the "very poor or no" job category (see Chart 5-1).

Year of Most Recent Injury. A number of questions were asked concerning the respondent's present physical condition, the number and kind of additional injuries and illnesses he had that kept him out of work, and his evaluation of the general level of his health. The year of the most recent injury to keep him out of work was found to have some association with whether or not he was in a "better" job, and to have a considerable association with whether or not he was in the "very poor or no" job category. There was no difference in these distributions between those whose most recent injury occurred in 1955 or 1956 and those whose most recent injury occurred before 1955. But the distribution among those who were injured in 1957 or later was substantially different, as is shown below:

	Year of injury		
	1950 to 1954	*1955 or 1956*	*1957 or later*
"Better" job category	46%	45%	34%
"Same or somewhat poorer" job category	39	40	37
"Very poor or no" job category	15	15	29
Total:	**100%**	**100%**	**100%**

This suggests that it takes several years—perhaps up to three or four—for many of the disabled men to recover sufficiently to be able to re-enter the labor market at a level of employment about as good as they are likely to have. This is strongly suggested by analysis of the men's reports of physical problems at time of interview, in relation to job category and year of injury, as follows:

49

Disabled Workers in the Labor Market

	Per cent of men reporting physical problems at time of interview (1960)[a]		
	Year of most recent injury		
	1950 to 1954	*1955 or 1956*	*1957 or later*
"Better" job category	18%	13%	50%
"Same or somewhat poorer" job category	21	18	52
"Very poor or no" job category	68	60	90

[a] Per cent of men within specified job category and time interval. Thus, for example, of all men injured in the period 1950-54 and who were in "better" jobs in 1960, 18 per cent reported physical problems (in 1960) whereas 82 per cent reported no such problems.

In short, it would appear that length of time since accident in relation to job category is relevant only within the recovery period. Once a man has recovered (as much as he ever will), additional time does not, by itself, place him in an improved job category.

Receipt of Medical Treatment. In line with the above, we find that those still receiving medical treatment (at the time of interview) were much less likely to be employed and, if employed, much less likely to have a better job than before.

Multiple Injuries and Chains. To fall in the category of "multiple injuries" the respondent had to have had two or more separate injuries, unrelated to each other, each of which caused him to be out of work for a period of at least a month.[6] The respondent with a "chain" injury, on the other hand, was one who had suffered an injury with at least one recurrence that had added to the original disability. Typical of a person with "multiple" injuries would be a respondent who broke his leg on one occasion, injured his back on another, and lost a finger on a third. Typical of a man with a "chain" injury would be a recurrent back case.

As might be expected, the more injuries, the less likely was the person to be employed, and if employed, the less likely was he to be among those with "better" jobs. The proportion in "better" jobs was 49 per cent of all those having only one injury, but it drops to 38 per cent for those with two, and down to 30 per cent for those with three or more injuries. The proportion who had "very poor or no" jobs rises in the opposite di-

---

[6] In a few cases radical changes in employment, such as having to change occupation, or work only part time, were accepted as substitutes for unemployment. See Chapter 1 on the construction of the summary groups and indexes.

50

Chart 5-1. PER CENT OF DISABLED MEN WHO HELD "BETTER" JOBS IN 1960, ACCORDING TO SELECTED CHARACTERISTICS OF THE MEN

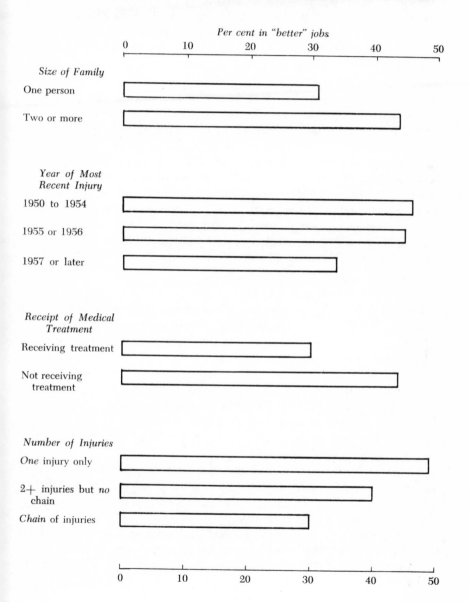

rection: from 15 per cent for those with one injury, to 19 per cent for those with two, to 30 per cent among those with three or more.

The same relationships—virtually the same relative percentages—obtain when we study chain injuries, and also when the experience of persons with chains is compared with that of persons who did not experience chain injuries but did experience multiples ones. Those with chain injuries were least likely to return to work: 32 per cent had "very poor or no" jobs as compared with 14 per cent for those who had only one injury and 18 per cent for those who had more than one, none of which was a chain.

Summary. The types of men most likely to be in the "better" job category were: those living in families of two or more persons (most of whom were married and living with their wives); those who had not been injured within three years prior to time of interview; those who were no longer receiving medical treatment; and those who had been injured only once. The families of the men in these "better" jobs had median annual incomes of $7,400.

SELF-EVALUATION OF CURRENT PHYSICAL
    AND EMOTIONAL CONDITION

Quality of Job. Those who gave a negative assessment of their present physical condition (i.e., said that they were often in pain or *volunteered* that they were disabled in answer to the question: How would you describe your present physical condition?) were far more likely to be in the "very poor or no" job category. For example, 29 per cent of those who said that they were often in pain were in the "very poor or no" job category, as compared with 15 per cent of all other men; 27 per cent of those who voluntarily mentioned their disabilities were in this category, versus 16 per cent of those who did not. (See Chart 5-2, showing negative assessment distribution by job group.)

Nearly half (43 per cent) of the men interviewed had either talked to a mental health worker concerning "nervous problems," or else, if they had not actually done so, thought that such a talk would have been helpful at some time during their lives.

Of the men reporting both physical and emotional problems, about half (51 per cent) had "very poor or no" jobs; and only 1 man in 5 was in a "better" job.[7] Of those with physical complaints *only*, a substantially

---

[7] See also Chapter 1, section on "Summary Groups and Indexes."

52

Chart 5-2. RELATIONSHIP OF LABOR PERFORMANCE TO MENTION OF SPECIFIED EMOTIONAL AND PHYSICAL DIFFICULTIES

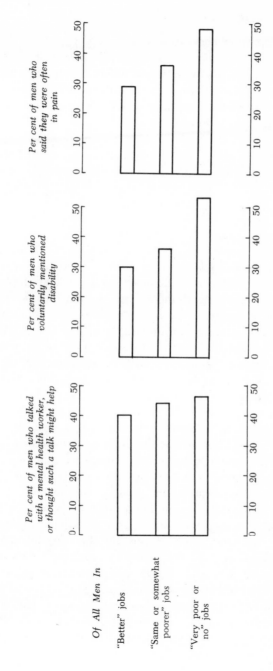

higher proportion had "very poor or no" jobs than did those who reported emotional difficulties *only* (25 per cent versus 9 per cent) (Chart 5-3). This fact reflects our earlier finding of a higher rate of nonemployment among those who were more recently injured, or who were still receiving medical treatment at the time of the interview. The percentages were as follows:

	"Better" jobs	*"Same or somewhat poorer" jobs*	*"Very poor or no" jobs*	*Total*
Reported some kind of difficulty	34%	37%	29%	100%
Physical and emotional	19	30	51	100
Physical only	42	33	25	100
Emotional only	44	47	9	100
No difficulty reported	53	41	6	100

Problems and "Relative Deprivation." On the basis of our findings concerning a respondent's financial condition and employment situation, no "relative deprivation" theory can explain the incidence of reporting a physical or emotional problem. Studying only the men with jobs, we find that among those earning wages of less than $100 a week, almost 2 out of 3 were likely to report some physical or emotional difficulty. However, among men earning $100 or over, fewer than half so reported. But their mentioning, or not mentioning, such difficulties was much more closely associated with absolute earnings than with the labor performance group they happened to be in. If his earnings were under $100 a week, the respondent in a "better" job was just as likely to report a physical or emotional problem as was the lower-wage worker who was in a "same or somewhat poorer" job. And the same is true among those in the $100 and over category. It is the absolute level of his wages, and not some kind of "relative deprivation," that is most associated with the fact of reporting a physical or emotional problem (Chart 5-4).

If "relative deprivation" were of any importance in this instance, it would be only as an explanation for the "deviant cases"—those lower-wage workers who did not report any such problems, and those higher-wage workers who did. Under such circumstances, among those with wages of $100 and over, the proportion reporting would have to be higher among those in the "same or somewhat poorer" jobs than among those in the "better" jobs. Correspondingly, of those with wages of less than $100, the proportion without complaints would have to be higher among

54

Chart 5-3. PER CENT OF DISABLED MEN WITH PARTICULAR KINDS OF COMPLAINTS WHO WERE IN "BETTER" JOBS AND IN "VERY POOR OR NO" JOBS IN 1960

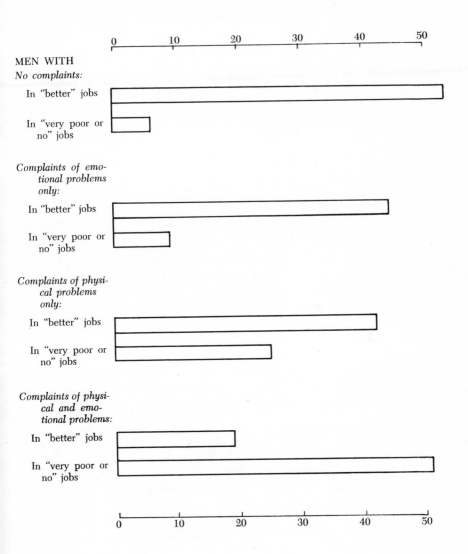

Chart 5-4.   PER CENT OF MEN IN SELECTED WAGE AND LABOR
PERFORMANCE GROUPS REPORTING PHYSICAL OR EMOTIONAL
PROBLEMS, OR BOTH

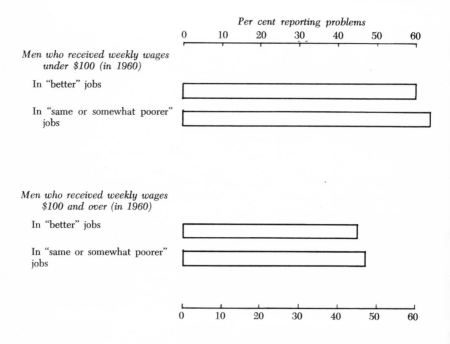

those in the "better" jobs than among those in the "same or somewhat poorer" jobs. Yet this was not the case. There was actually no difference, within either of the two wage groups, between those in the "better" jobs and those in the "same or somewhat poorer" jobs. Insofar as wages and job stability are related to mention of physical or emotional conditions, it is the absolute wage level, not the wage level relative to what it was at the time of injury, that bears the actual relationship.

Ability to Work. One out of 4 of the men in our study reported no chronic limitation on his activities as a result of his injury. Forty-seven per cent reported being limited to some extent in the kinds of jobs they could perform; 23 per cent said they were limited in non-job activities only (sports, eating, climbing, etc.). Only 5 per cent claimed to be unable to work at all. So far as this assessment by the respondent of his ability to work is concerned, we find the following:

Extent of limitation	*Per cent in "very poor or no" category*
Cannot work at all at present time	100%
Can work, but limited in amount or kind of work	23
Can work, but limited in amount or kind of other activities	11
Not limited in any of these ways	7

Since we used exactly the same question with regard to chronic limitation affecting major activity[8] as does the United States National Health Survey, we can compare our findings directly with those of this survey. Furthermore, the National Health Survey classifies the respondents as "working (or not working) at time limitation of major activity started"[9] and as "usually (or not usually) working at the time of interview."[10] In short, the proportion of National Health Survey respondents who were working at the time limitation started is approxmately equivalent to

---

[8] "Chronic activity limitation affecting major activity" includes men who "cannot work at all at present" and "can work but limited in amount or kind of work."

[9] Based on the National Health Survey question, "Were you at work at your job or business when the accident happened?"

[10] Based on the National Health Survey question, "What were you doing most of the past 12 months?" The possible answers are: working, looking for work, keeping house, going to school, something else. A subsidiary question asked was: "Are you retired?"

Disabled Workers in the Labor Market

our workmen's compensation group; and those who were not usually working at the time of the National Health Survey interview are approximately equivalent to our group of men in "very poor or no" jobs.

Finally, the National Health Survey data are available for men whose duration of limitation was five or more years, which compares somewhat with the fact that in our study the men had received their limitation about five years before the time of interview. The comparisons are as follows:

National Health Survey[a]	*Per cent not usually working, or per cent in "very poor or no" job category*
Men aged 25 to 54 years, total	26% not usually working
Duration of limitation 5+ years	24% not usually working
Our study	20% in "very poor or no" job category

a From unpublished table kindly furnished by the U. S. National Health Survey; period covered, July 1959 through June 1960.

Considering the fact that our study is reasonably comparable to, though not identical with, the National Health Survey, the similarity of findings strongly suggests that the employment experiences of men in the New York Metropolitan Area are similar to those of all men in the United States. (For further information see Appendix B.)

Estimates of the Future. Those who were in "better" jobs were far more optimistic than the others in their estimates of what their physical condition would be like five years from the date of interview. Those who were in the "very poor or no" job category were the most pessimistic. A similar relationship was found in answer to the question on future work opportunities. Those in the "better" jobs thought they would do even better in the future. Those who had experienced the greatest loss ("very poor or no" job group) were most pessimistic: about half of them said either that they did not know, or that they thought their future work opportunities would be worse than they already were. Only 1 in 4 of those in the intermediate category ("same or somewhat poorer") were this pessimistic about the future.

58

Part II

ATTEMPTS TO PREDICT FUTURE EXPERIENCES IN THE LABOR MARKET

[6]

Pivotal Importance of First Job Following Accident

In the previous chapters we examined in detail the employment status and characteristics of these disabled men as of the time of the interview (including the year preceding the interview). The information on non-employment (Chapters 3 and 4) referred to a man's employment status as of the time of the interview; for most men this was sometime in 1960. The information on quality of job (Chapter 5) referred to the nature of the employment which the man had during the year preceding the interview. As we saw, the majority of the men who had "very poor or no" jobs in the year preceding, were also unemployed as of the time of interview.[1]

Now one crucial question from the viewpoint of vocational rehabilitation and re-employment programs is: at the time of the workmen's compensation accident, can we predict which man five years later is most likely to have made such a poor adjustment to the labor market that special rehabilitation and re-employment efforts should be made on his behalf? And, conversely, which one is likely to make a successful adjustment without the aid of special rehabilitation efforts? The services of rehabilitation and re-employment agencies may be facilitated to the extent that such predictions can be made successfully.

In this and the following chapter we shall examine a number of characteristics of the man and of his job as of the time of injury, or shortly

---

[1] See also Appendix A, Table A.3.

61

thereafter, in an effort to predict future labor market performance. In doing this we shall concentrate on quality of job and try to predict, in particular, those who will be found in the "very poor or no" job category. If we are able to predict this group, we shall have pointed to those who are most in need of special rehabilitation and re-employment efforts.

When we speak of predicting future performance in the labor market, we are speaking of a period about five years after the accident. For this is the average number of years between the time of the workmen's compensation injury which brought the man into our study and the time of interview. If we may assume that the factors which operated during the latter half of the 1950s, resulting in better adjustment to the labor market on the part of some than of others, will continue to operate in the future, then our predictions should be of some relevancy.

When we speak of the "characteristics of the man and his job as of the time of the injury," we are thinking of those factors about which information is commonly obtained at the time of the workmen's compensation hearings or shortly thereafter. Information is routinely collected in many jurisdictions on such factors as age, occupation and industry in which employed, name of firm, weekly earnings, the man's physical condition and medical history, nature of injury, etc. In addition, education or amount of schooling can be determined very easily at the time of the workmen's compensation hearings, and race or ethnic group can be and should be noted. Finally, it is feasible to follow the man to the time when he first returns to work and ascertain whether or not he went back to work for his former firm. All this information is often available at the time of the hearings (since such hearings are often held several months, or longer, after the accident has occurred).

On the basis of such information, what predictions can be made? In this chapter we are concentrating on one factor, whether the man did or did not return to the same firm in which he was employed at the time of the injury, since this factor seems to be of overriding importance. In the following chapter we shall consider a number of the other factors simultaneously, in an effort to make the best prediction possible.

RETURNING TO WORK

Length of Time Not Employed. About 1 man in 20 of those whom we studied never returned to work following the injury in which he became disabled. More precisely, he had not returned to work as of the time we interviewed him (on the average, some five years following the injury). Whether any of these men will yet return to work we do not know.[2]

Of those who returned to employment, almost 2 men in 3 returned within six months following injury. The distribution by number of months between jobs is as follows:

Months between jobs	*Per cent*
3 months or less	39
4 through 6 months	26
7 through 12 months	18
1 year up to 2 years	9
2 years or longer	8
Total:	**100%**

The reader must bear in mind that the above table includes the time required for physical recovery following the injury, as well as any time which may have been spent looking for work. Unfortunately, we were unable to distinguish between these two periods during the course of the interviews. Apparently for most of the respondents the distinction was blurred; if the informant went to a hospital he could tell us when he was discharged, but found it impossible to draw a meaningful line between time spent in physical recuperation and time spent in job seeking. Accordingly, in the preceding table we contented ourselves with measuring the total time elapsed between jobs.

Of the men who returned to work for the same firm, almost 4 in 5 went back to work within six months; but of those who found employment in different firms (including those who became self-employed), this proportion was fewer than 2 in 5 (Chart 6-1). Some of the reasons for this difference will be examined subsequently.[3]

Returning to the Same Firm. Two-thirds of the men we interviewed returned to the same firm[4]; 29 per cent went to work for a different firm or became self-employed; and only 6 per cent never went back to work. Of the two-thirds who went back to work for the same firm, 3 men in 5

---

2 See Chapter 12 for information on how many men think that they may return to work at some future (post-1960) date.

3 See Chapter 10.

4 An almost identical proportion was found in a study of the employment status of industrially injured workers in California, six to nine months after injury. See California State Department of Education, *The Vocational Rehabilitation of Industrially Injured Workers,* 1961, Table 10, p. 114.

Chart 6-1. MONTHS NOT EMPLOYED BETWEEN TIME OF INJURY
AND FIRST RETURN TO WORK, FOR MEN WHO DID, OR DID NOT,
RETURN TO WORK FOR SAME FIRM

Per cent who returned to work for *same* firm

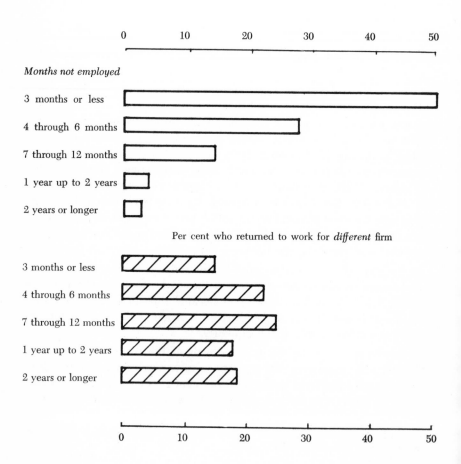

were still working there at the date of interview, some five years later. Of those whose first job after recovery was with a different firm, hardly any (perhaps 2 per cent) ended up returning to the firm they had worked for at the time of injury. In short, once they returned to the same employer there was a strong tendency to stay; once employed elsewhere, they never went back.

RELATION BETWEEN RETURNING TO SAME FIRM
AND IMPROVING ONE'S JOB

Quality of Job Held at Time of Interview. Those who returned to the same firm were about half again as likely to have a "better" job five years later as were those who did not (48 per cent as against 32 per cent). Also they were far less likely to have a "very poor or no" job (12 per cent as against 33 per cent). Those who were still working for the same firm at the time of interview had fared the best. Forty-nine per cent of them had better jobs and only 6 per cent were in the "very poor or no" job category (Chart 6-2).

We can summarize this factor by noting that, of the men in the "very poor or no" job category, two-thirds had failed to return to work for the same firm for which they had worked at the time of injury. Among all the men in our study, however, less than one-third had failed to return to work for the same firm.

Wages at Time of Interview. Whether the disabled worker returns to the same firm is an excellent predictor also of the direction of any possible change in weekly earnings over a period of approximately five years following his injury. Of those who returned to the same firm, nearly 9 out of 10 (86 per cent) received wages in 1960 above those they had been receiving at the time of injury. But the corresponding figure among those who went to a different firm (including those who became self-employed) was only 55 per cent. Thus, at the time of interview, 6 men in 10 who had reported decreases in wages (since the time of injury) had gone to work for a different firm.

The difference between the two groups started almost as soon as the worker went back to work following his injury. Of those who returned to the same firm, 91 per cent went back at the same or a higher wage, and only 9 per cent at a lower wage. But among those who did not return to the same firm, a total of 54 per cent went back to work at a *lower* wage.

Chart 6-2. QUALITY OF JOB HELD AT TIME OF INTERVIEW FOR MEN WHO DID, OR DID NOT, RETURN TO WORK FOR SAME FIRM

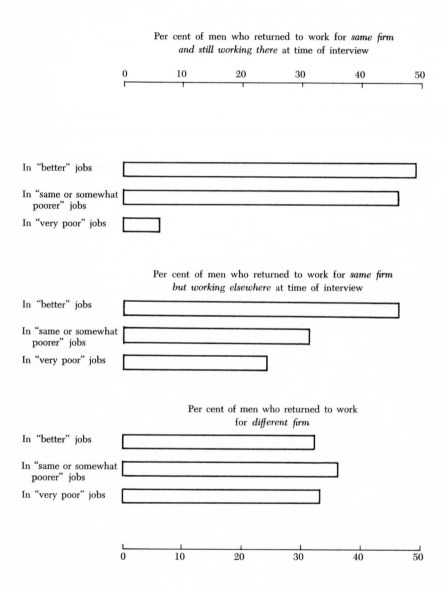

Once the pattern of higher or lower wages was established, there was little deviation from it; nor was there much difference between the two employment groups—those who returned to the same firm and those who did not. In both, only about 1 man out of 10 who went back at the same or higher wage later experienced a decrease. In either group, only 1 out of 4 who went back at a decrease later succeeded in obtaining an increase sufficient to put his earnings (at time of interview) above what they had been at the time of injury. Altogether, over 8 in 10 of those who returned to the same firm received and kept an increase in wages, while only 4 in 10 of those who went to a different firm succeeded in doing so (Charts 6-3 & 6-4). On the other hand, only 1 man in 20 of those who returned to the same firm received and kept a *decrease* in wages, while fully 4 in 10 of those who went to a different employer experienced this kind of loss.

Whether or not the first job after injury was with the same firm or a different one, the great preponderance of those who received wage *increases* kept them up to the time of interview, and the great preponderance of those who received wage *decreases* did likewise. But since the proportion receiving increases was twice as high among those who returned to the same firm as among those who went elsewhere, and since we know from other studies that involuntary job changes are more often accompanied by a wage loss than are voluntary changes, it seems highly probable that a large proportion of those who took jobs in other firms did so involuntarily. As we shall review subsequently, over half of the men who went to work for a different firm did so involuntarily.[5]

These changes in wages between time of injury and interview resulted in higher weekly earnings for the men who returned to work for the same firm as compared with those who returned to work for a different firm. The former had median earnings of $111 per week, and the latter only $86.

What is most significant is that at the time of injury, there was little difference in the weekly wages between the two groups. Those who subsequently returned to work for the same firm had earned at the time of injury a median wage of $96, as compared with one of $90 for those who subsequently went to work for a different firm.

---

[5] See Chapter 10.

67

Chart 6-3. CHANGE IN WEEKLY WAGES BETWEEN TIME OF INJURY
AND FIRST RETURN TO WORK, FOR MEN WHO DID, OR DID NOT,
RETURN TO WORK FOR SAME FIRM

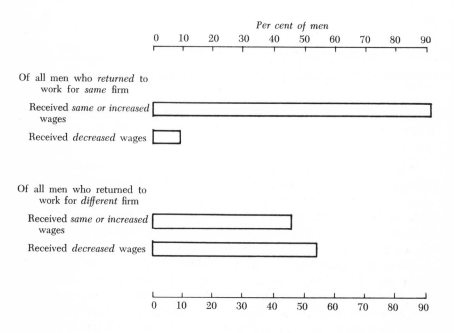

Steadiness of Employment. Another measure of the quality of a job
is the amount of employment which it provides over an extended period
of time. Previously we reviewed the quality of the jobs held by these
disabled men in terms of: (1) the number of weeks (and hours per
week) of employment during the year preceding the time of interview,
and (2) the weekly wages received. Now let us examine these jobs in
terms of the number of months they were employed during the *three*
years preceding the interview.

The relationship between steadiness of employment in the three years
preceding the interview (1960) and first returning to work for the same
or different firm is as follows:

68

Importance of First Job Following Accident

Months without work in the three years preceding interview	Per cent whose first job following injury was with	
	Same firm	Different firm[a]
Under 1 month	51%	30%
1 to 6 months	32	17
7 to 12 months	11	13
13 to 24 months	4	13
25 months or more	2	27
Total	**100%**	**100%**

[a] Includes those who never returned to work.

Clearly, if the disabled man is rehired by the same firm for which he worked at the time of injury, he is much more likely to have steady employment in future years than if he must seek a job in a different firm.

Chart 6-4. CHANGE IN WEEKLY WAGES BETWEEN TIME OF INJURY AND TIME OF INTERVIEW, FOR MEN WHO DID, OR DID NOT, RETURN TO WORK FOR SAME FIRM

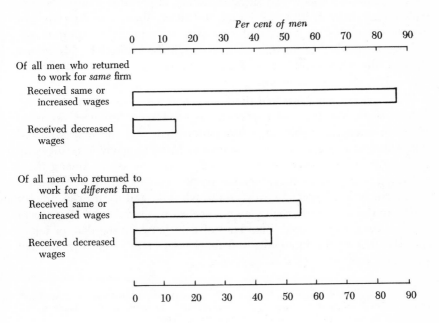

69

Indeed, of all the men who had been out of work for a year or longer in the three years preceding the time of interview, two-thirds had not returned to work for the same firm for which they had worked at the time of injury.

THE RELEVANCE OF OCCUPATION

Changing firms and changing occupations are almost concurrent events. Of those who returned to the same firm in their first job after injury, 80 per cent went back to the same occupation; but only 25 per cent of those who went to a different firm (or into self-employment) went back to same occupation.[6] Was this because those who went to different firms were physically unable to perform the tasks connected with their former occupations? Our data provide only a clue. To be sure, only 31 per cent of those who went to *different* firms expressed confidence that they could do the jobs they had at the time of injury about as well afterwards as before. Yet this proportion among men who returned to the *same* firms was only slightly higher: 38 per cent. The majority of men in both groups expressed doubts about their physical ability to perform well in the jobs which they held at time of injury. In short, then, our data do not prove that ability to perform the work is an especially important determinant of whether an injured worker will be rehired by his former firm; on the other hand, our data do not prove that ability to perform is ignored by the prospective employer.

Whatever he may have told the interviewer about his ability to do his former work, the man who returned to his former firm was far more likely to continue in his same occupation than was the man who did not. And continuing in this occupation was far more likely to result in an increase in wages, whether or not the firm was the same. Among those returning to the same occupation, the proportionate gains in weekly earnings were little different between those who did and those who did not return to the same firm. Eighty-eight per cent of the first and 80 per cent of the second experienced some kind of gain between the date of injury and the date of the interview; and for 4 men in 10 in each group that gain amounted to at least $20 a week.

---

[6] In the California study (California State Department of Education, *The Vocational Rehabilitation of Industrially Injured Workers*) these proportions were 82 per cent and 36 per cent, respectively (Table 10, p. 114).

70

Chart 6-5. OCCUPATION AT TIME OF INJURY AND TIME OF INTERVIEW, FOR MEN WHO DID, OR DID NOT, RETURN TO WORK FOR SAME FIRM

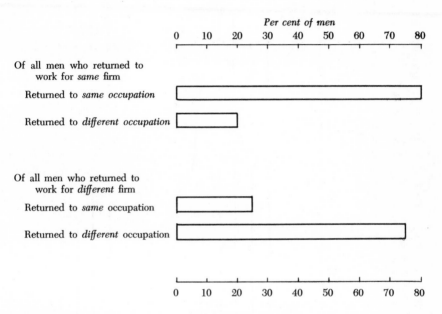

The major difference between the two employment groups was among those who did not return to their former occupations. Men who changed occupations were less likely to have received higher wages (by the time of interview) and more likely to have received lower wages than were those who went back to work at their former occupations. The differences between those who remained in their former occupations and those who left them were much greater among men who had changed firms. In fact, the men who suffered the greatest losses were those who changed *both* occupation and firm. Among these men, about half reported decreases in weekly wages and half reported increases. This appears to be a mixed group. Those who improved their jobs by changing both firm and occupation, we suspect, were largely voluntary changers. On the

Chart 6-6. CHANGE IN WAGES BETWEEN TIME OF INJURY AND TIME OF INTERVIEW, IN RELATION TO CHANGE IN OCCUPATION AND FIRM BETWEEN TIME OF INJURY AND FIRST RETURN TO WORK

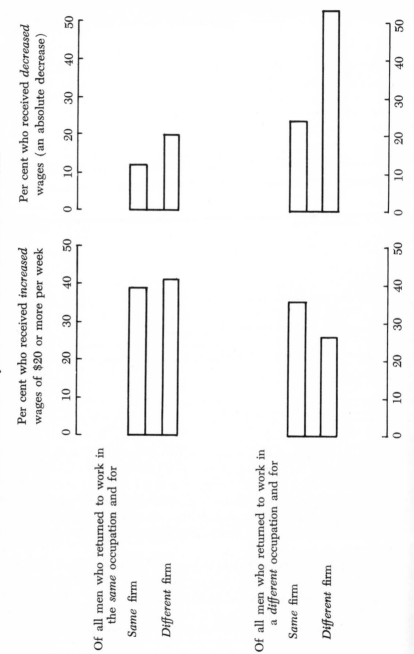

other hand, those who suffered decreases in wages, we suspect, were largely men who were forced to change occupation and firm in order to find employment. (Charts 6-5 and 6-6.)

In short, whether or not the disabled worker held his own or improved his job situation was related somewhat more to whether he had been able to remain in the same occupation than to whether or not he went back to the same firm. But his being able to remain in that same occupation was related, to a very considerable extent, to whether he was re-hired by his firm.

SUMMARY

Whatever measure we use of relative success or failure in the labor market some five years following injury, we find it closely related to the circumstances of the disabled man's first job following his return to work. If his firm (as of the time of injury) hires him back, he is assured of relative success in the future labor market. And this assurance is increased if he can return to work at the same occupation which he held at the time of his injury.

Those who went back to the same employer were likely to stay with him; those who did not were almost certain to remain out of his employ. Those who went back at a higher wage were likely to remain at a higher wage; those who went back at a lower wage were likely to remain at a lower one. Yet, over all, those who went to work for the same firm did far better than those who went to work for a different firm. In part, this seems to have been because they were much more likely to remain in the same occupational category—a possibly important determinant of seniority rights, promotion possibilities, and so on. It may also have been important from the standpoint of providing a fairly friendly, familiar, and, possibly, sympathetic setting in which to re-adjust to working.

Upon their recovery, some two-thirds of the disabled men in our study returned to work for the same firm for which they had been working, while one-third sought—or were forced to seek—new employment. This one-third, however, comprised two-thirds of all the men who ultimately made a poor adjustment to the labor market. In short, it would appear that the large majority of the disabled men who may ultimately need rehabilitation because of relative failure in the labor market can be picked out at an early date.

73

[7]

Predicting the Job Failures

Since rehabilitation should be most concerned with those men who fail to obtain reasonably suitable employment—including those who are unable to obtain any employment—the ability to pick out such men at the time of their workmen's compensation injury, or soon thereafter, is highly important. Such predictions would permit the rehabilitation agencies to concentrate their efforts on those most in need of rehabilitation. How well, then, can we predict failure in the job market some five years after the injury? In this chapter we shall continue our efforts, commenced in Chapter 6, to predict those men who will be in "very poor or no" jobs, on the basis of the information known at the time of the injury.

In Chapter 6 we saw that an extremely important indicator was whether or not the man returned to work for his former firm. We also determined that about one-third of the men failed to return to work for their previous firms, and that this group included about two-thirds of all the men who were found to be in the "very poor or no" job category. Is there other information about the man that we could use to improve our predictions? In this chapter we shall introduce these factors: the man's age; whether or not the injury at the time of the workmen's compensation accident was a chain injury; the amount of education which the man had; whether he had been employed in a white-collar or manu-

75

al occupation; and his ethnic group. All these will be considered in relation to whether or not he returned to work for the same firm for which he had worked at the time of his injury. All of these factors will now be considered simultaneously.

Before presenting our findings, we wish to remind our readers that we are here concerned with *indicators*, rather than *causes* or explanations. Indeed, the single most important indicator—whether or not the man returned to work for the same firm—in itself tells us nothing about *why* some men return to the same firm and others do not. In Chapter 10 we shall examine this problem within the limits of our study; but a fuller explanation can emerge only from a special study designed to elicit such information.

Another indicator, age, tells us comparatively little about any causes, except that personnel men are often prejudiced against older job applicants. Age in itself is not necessarily a "cause" of poor job performance; it may or may not be, depending on a great many other considerations involving both the man and the job.[1] Nevertheless, age is a useful indicator. In similar fashion, education, ethnic group, and other characteristics to be considered are useful indicators but not necessarily "explanations."

FACTORS KNOWN TO BE ASSOCIATED WITH
PERFORMANCE IN THE LABOR MARKET

Let us first review the distribution of job categories separately, considering each characteristic as of the time of injury. Subsequently we shall review the characteristics in combination. In general, the men who tended to be found in the "very poor or no" job category in 1960 were: those who did not return to work for the same firm; those with chain injuries (as of the time of the accident); those aged 45 and over (at the time of the interview); those who had only eight or less years of schooling; those who were operatives or laborers or service workers; and those who were Negro or Puerto Rican.

---

[1] See *Demonstration of Feasibility of Vocational Rehabilitation for Vocationally Handicapped Persons 60 Years of Age and Over,* Second Annual Progress Report, New York, Federation Employment and Guidance Service, 1959. See also, Tobias Wagner, *Selective Job Placement,* The National Conservation Bureau, 1946.

The distributions by job categories are as follows:

	"Better" job	"Same or somewhat poorer" job	"Very poor or no" job	Total
Returned to same firm	48%	39%	13%	100%
Did not return to same firm	31	37	32	100
Injury other than chain	44	39	17	100
Chain injury	26	37	37	100
9 years or more of schooling	48	37	15	100
8 years or less of schooling	31	41	28	100
White-collar or craft occupation	43	42	15	100
Operative, laborer, service worker	38	38	24	100
White (excluding Puerto Rican)	44	39	17	100
Negro and Puerto Rican	24	38	38	100

These characteristics are all interrelated to some extent, but the relationships are not very high. For example, in relating age and education we find that among men under age 45, 21 per cent had eight years or less of schooling; among men aged 45 and over, 51 per cent had that amount of education; the correlation of these two variables is - .31.

Accordingly, in order to study the possible influence of each characteristic separately, we cross-tabulated each characteristic by all other characteristics, within the limits imposed by the numbers of cases. The analyses to be presented are: 1) Men with chain injuries, cross-tabulated by age and by whether or not they returned to work for the same firm; 2) men who did not have a chain injury, cross-tabulated by age, by education, by occupational grouping, and by whether or not they returned to work for the same firm. Because of the small number of cases, ethnic characteristic was excluded, although the possible influence of this factor is considered subsequently.

MEN WITH CHAIN INJURIES

Of all men whose workmen's compensation injury was a recurrence of a previous injury, 37 per cent were found to be in the "very poor or no" job category at the time of interview. The proportions in this job category in the two age groups and among those who returned to work for the same firm, as compared with those who did not return, are as follows:

77

	Under age 45	Age 45 and over
Returned to same firm	9%	15%
Did not return to same firm*	43	71
Total:	**22**	**56**

* Includes "never returned to work."

Clearly, age is important (the difference between 22 per cent and 56 per cent is statistically significant).[2] But also, returning or not returning to work for the former firm remains of overriding importance as a predictor of labor market behavior some five years subsequent to the accident.

Now we should note that one-quarter of those who have chain injuries and who are in the "very poor or no" job category are men who never returned to work following their injury. Hence, we may ask: how well did the men who did return to work fare in the labor market as of the time of the interview (1960)? The proportions of men with and without chain injuries, in the "very poor or no" job category, are as follows:

	Chain injury	Non-chain injury
Returned to same firm	11%	13%
Returned to different firm*	19	18
All men	14	14

* Excludes "never returned to work."

Apparently, if the man does return to work following his injury, it makes no difference whether or not he had a chain injury so far as his job situation is concerned five years later. It is possible that those persons with chain injuries who did return to work were less physically disadvantaged than those who did not. Also, they may have been injured in such a way that recurrences seemed less likely. But other possibilities are suggested by two factors: the unfavorable attitudes on the part of employers toward those kinds of injuries most likely to be chains; and the data on voluntary non-return to the old firm (the considerable proportion failing even to contact the old firm) (see Chapter 10). Both employers and injured men may perceive certain kinds of injuries as

---

2 Standardizing the two age groups on the basis of the same numbers returning to, or not returning to, the same firm, alters the proportions as follows: under age 45, 27 per cent in the "very poor or no" job category; age 45 and over, 45 per cent.·

those most likely to recur; but they may fail to perceive that over-all performance over a period of time may not be greatly affected by such recurrences. Our data appear to suggest this possibility by the relatively creditable record of those men with chain injuries who did manage to get employed following the injury which brought them to our attention.

Whatever the reason for returning or not returning to work for the same firm may be, if the man does return to work for the same firm he is less likely to be in the "very poor or no" job category.[3] This finding suggests that it should be possible to select out those men who will have employment trouble in the future, particularly if the full medical information about them is taken into consideration. On the basis of our very imperfect medical information—namely, that the man had a chain injury—together with information on whether or not he returned to work for the same firm, we were able to pick out many of the men who subsequently had employment problems. But if full medical information (as of the time of the workmen's compensation hearing) were brought to bear, even more accurate prediction should be possible.

Now it can be argued that those men who show a high probability of having employment problems in the future are the very ones who should receive the maximum attention from rehabilitation agencies.[4] Whether they can or cannot be satisfactorily rehabilitated, we have no way of knowing.

MEN WITH OTHER THAN CHAIN INJURIES

For the majority of the men, the injury suffered at the time of the workmen's compensation accident was unrelated to any previous injury (according to the respondents). We have enough cases of such men to permit simultaneous analysis by whether or not they returned to work for the same firm (as of the time of the accident), by age, by education, and by major occupational group (white-collar and crafts; operatives, laborers, or service workers). The proportions of the men in each subcategory who were found to be in the "very poor or no" job category at the time of the interview, were as follows:

---

[3] There were not enough cases among those with chain injuries to permit analysis by age.

[4] See Chapter 8, "Job Training," which discusses the extent to which persons in our study received vocational training services subsequent to their injuries.

Disabled Workers in the Labor Market

Characteristics	No. of cases	Per cent in "very poor or no" job category
Under age 45 (at interview)		
8 years or less of schooling		
white-collar or craft occupations		
returned to work for same firm	9	°
did not return to work for same firm	9	°
operatives, laborers, service workers		
returned to work for same firm	26	15
did not return to work for same firm	28	29
9 years or more of schooling		
white-collar or craft occupations		
returned to work for the same firm	118	4
did not return to work for same firm	48	10
operatives, laborers, service workers		
returned to work for the same firm	72	10
did not return to work for same firm	42	17
Age 45 and over (at interview)		
8 years or less of schooling		
white-collar or craft occupations		
returned to work for same firm	43	21
did not return to work for same firm	28	25
operatives, laborers, service workers		
returned to work for same firm	67	28
did not return to work for same firm	43	44
9 years or more of schooling		
white-collar or craft occupations		
returned to work for same firm	73	12
did not return to work for same firm	32	38
operatives, laborers, service workers		
returned to work for same firm	45	9
did not return to work for same firm	26	31

° No percentage shown on base of fewer than 25 cases.

Returning to work for the same firm. Examination of these rates for the several sub-categories reveals that in every instance there was a smaller proportion in the "very poor or no" job category among those whose initial job after recovery was with the same firm for which they had worked at the time of the injury. We can standardize these several sub-categories so that each of the two groups—those who did and did not return to the same firm—will have the same distribution by age, edu-

80

cation, and occupational group. When this is done it is seen that the standardized proportion of those who returned to the same firm, but eventually ended in the "very poor or no" job category, is 13 per cent, as compared with 25 per cent of those who did not return to work for the same firm.

Age. We have already seen that a larger proportion of the men aged 45 and over, as compared with younger men, were in the "very poor or no" job category. Examination of the proportions found in this employment group among the various sub-categories reveals that in five instances the proportion was smaller among the younger men. For example, let us consider men who had nine years or more of schooling, were in white-collar or craft occupations, and returned to work for the same firm; among those under 45 years of age only 4 per cent were in the "very poor or no" job category, whereas among the older men 12 per cent were in this job category.

The only exception to this pattern is found among men who had nine or more years of schooling, returned to work for the same firm and were operatives, laborers, or service workers; among those men under age 45, 10 per cent were in the "very poor or no" job category as compared with 9 per cent among men aged 45 and over. Since this is the only exception, we can consider age as an important characteristic, even after taking into account education, occupational group, and whether or not the man returned to work for the same firm. Furthermore, since we are here analyzing only men who did not have chain injuries, we are also, in effect, taking type of injury into account.

The several sub-categories can be standardized so that each of the two groups—those under 45 years of age and those aged 45 and over— will have the same distribution by education, occupational group, and whether or not they returned to work for the same firm. Making these computations reveals that among men under 45 years of age, 10 per cent were in the "very poor or no" job category, and among the older men, 23 per cent. Clearly, increasing age indicates increasingly difficult employment problems for many men.

Education. A larger proportion of men with little schooling (i.e., eight years or less), were in the "very poor or no" job category than of the better educated men. This was found to be the case in all but one instance (see tabulation on p. 80). Among men who were 45 years of age and over, who were in white-collar or craft occupations and had

Disabled Workers in the Labor Market

not returned to work for the same firm, there were only 25 per cent in the "very poor or no" job category among men with lesser schooling, and 38 per cent among men with more schooling. In all other instances the higher rates were found among the more poorly educated men, indicating that lack of education contributed to their employment difficulties.

Again we can standardize so that the two groups—those with but eight years or less of schooling and those with nine years or more—will have the same distribution by age, occupational group, and whether or not they returned to work for the same firm. When this is done, we find that among the more poorly educated 19 per cent were in the "very poor or no" job category, as compared with 14 per cent among the better educated. Education still seems to have some influence, but not as much as age or returning to work for the same firm.

Major occupational groups. These are the two divisions: (1) white-collar and craft occupations, and (2) operatives, laborers, and service workers. In general, the first group contains the higher paying jobs and those which require somewhat more education and skills. Some of the jobs in the second group, particularly the jobs of laborers, sometimes provide only casual or intermittent employment.

There is some tendency for men who held occupations in the first group at the time of the workmen's compensation accident, to have somewhat lower proportions in the "very poor or no" job category at the time of interview. This relationship does not appear to be too significant, however, since in two instances there were higher proportions of men with "very poor or no" jobs in the white-collar and craft group. This was the case among men aged 45 and over who had nine years or more of schooling, both among those who returned to work for the same firm and those who did not. On the other hand, there were but four instances in which the lower proportions in "very poor or no" jobs were found among the white-collar and craft workers (see table p. 80).

Summary. From the preceding analysis (excluding those with chains at the time of their injury) it follows that the men for whom we would predict the most difficult employment situation some five years after injury should be those 45 years of age and over, with eight years or less of schooling, who did not return to work for the same firm, and who were either operatives, laborers, or service workers. Among such men we find that 44 per cent were in the "very poor or no" job category.

This, in fact, is the highest proportion observed in any of the categories previously analysed.

Conversely, the men for whom we would predict the best employment situation should be younger men with more education, who returned to work for the same firm, and who were white-collar workers. Among this group we find that only 4 per cent were in the "very poor or no" job category at the time of the interview.

INCLUSION OF MEN WITH CHAIN INJURIES
IN THE PREDICTION EQUATION

We saw previously that men whose workmen's compensation injury was a chain faced a much more difficult employment problem. Many of them never returned to work following their injury, and altogether 37 per cent were found to be in the "very poor or no" job category at the time of the interview. Now, let us combine chain injury with the characteristics just studied: age, education, and return to work for the same firm. When this is done we find that our prediction is far more precise. Almost three-quarters of the men who had chain injuries, were aged 45 or above, did not return to work for the same firm, and had but eight years or less of schooling, were found to be in the "very poor or no" job category.

Statistically, this prediction is very satisfying. From the viewpoint of actually selecting men who will have a difficult time making a suitable employment adjustment, however, this prediction leaves something to be desired, since only about 2 per cent of all the men have this combination of characteristics. Hence, only a small portion of the men who should receive rehabilitation are picked out (at the time of injury or shortly thereafter) on the basis of these characteristics in combination. To have more practical value, our prediction equation should select out a much larger proportion of the men who will have employment problems in the years following their injury, and who therefore should receive rehabilitation.

ETHNIC CHARACTERISTICS

Because of the small number of cases in the study, only limited analysis can be made of the possible usefulness of this factor as an indicator of future employment. The two factors of overriding importance which we have just examined are: returning or not returning to work for the same firm, and having or not having a chain injury. Therefore, let us eliminate the influence of these two factors and see if there is any remaining influence which might be attributable to ethnic group.

We divided our men into two ethnic groups: white (excluding Puerto Rican), and Negro and Puerto Rican combined. The reason for this is simply that the Negro and Puerto Rican men in the general population seem to have more difficulties in obtaining employment; if this is also true among the men we studied, then ethnic characteristics should emerge as relevant elements for indicating future job adjustment.

Men in both ethnic groups who had chain injuries were more likely to be found in the "very poor or no" job category, as follows:

	Chain injury	*Non-chain injury*
White	33%	15%
Negro and Puerto Rican	66	35

Let us now subdivide the men who did not have chain injuries into two groups: those who did, and those who did not, return to work for the same firm. We now find the following proportions in the "very poor or no" job category:

	Returned to same firm	*Did not return to same firm*
White	10%	22%
Negro and Puerto Rican	31	40

Although we are unable to take age, education, and occupation into account, it would seem that ethnic characteristics, in themselves, are indicators of relatively poor job adjustment in the future.

SCREENING PROSPECTIVE REHABILITATION CLIENTS

We have seen that several factors are important in indicating whether a man will ultimately make such a poor labor market adjustment that early vocational rehabilitation efforts would apparently be necessary. No one factor of those considered here is, by itself, a conclusive indicator. How, then, might these factors be grouped so that, at the time of the injury or shortly thereafter, the men who probably will require special rehabilitation efforts can be selected?

Of all the men studied, 1 in 5 ultimately was found to be in the "very poor or no" job category, indicating a poor adjustment to the labor market. Let us now try to narrow down the group to be reviewed, in an effort to describe the smallest sized group of workmen's compensation cases

84

which will contain the largest number of men who will end up in the "very poor or no" job category.

1) Consider all men whose injuries are recurrences of earlier injuries; about one-quarter of all men in the "very poor or no" job category are men with such chain injuries.[5] Include other men who are judged to be "very seriously" injured, on the basis of the medical examination at the time of the workmen's compensation hearing—a group whom we could not designate on the basis of the data available to us.

2) Of the remaining men—those whom we designated as men with non-chain injuries—consider all those who did not return to work for the same firm for which they had worked at the time of accident. This group includes about 4 in 10 of all men in the "very poor or no" job category.

3) Of the remaining men, consider all those aged 45 and over, and who also had only eight years or less of schooling. This group includes about 2 in 10 of all men in the "very poor or no" job category.

Altogether, the preceding three groups contained a little over half of the men in our study but over 80 per cent of the men who (at the time of interview) were in the "very poor or no" job category.[6] The efficiency of this selection process can be judged from the proportions of each screeening group in the "very poor or no" job category, as follows:

	Per cent of men in each successive "screening group" who also are in the "Very poor or no" job category
1) All men with chain injuries (recurrences of previous injuries)	37%
2) Of remaining, those who did not return to work for same firm as of time of accident	26
3) Of remaining, those aged 45+ who also had but 8 years or less of schooling	25
4) All other men	10

---

[5] Subsequent to the injury that brought them into our sample, about 15 per cent more of the men in the "very poor or no" job category had an injury that brought them into the "chain" category (see table on p. 16).

[6] Of course we could not give our men a medical exam which would assess their physical condition five years, on an average, prior to the date of interview. In actuality, if full advantage were taken of all medical data available at the time of injury, the prediction should be considerably more precise than our 80 per cent location of the most serious future problems.

Additional refinements in the screening process are possible by paying extra attention to Negro and Puerto Rican men in the "all other" group, and to younger men with eight years or less of schooling who were in unskilled jobs at the time of their workmen's compensation accident and were earning well below average wages. Although our data did not permit examining men with these characteristics carefully enough to evaluate the exact relevancy of these characteristics to subsequent job adjustment, our data do suggest that these two additional characteristics warrant special attention during a screening process.

Furthermore, information should be available at the time of the injury, indicating the probability of the man returning to work for the same firm. The policies of the firm, the man's seniority, the activities of labor unions, and perhaps other information, in addition to the indicators which we just examined, will help decide whether the man probably will or will not return to the same firm. The probable need for vocational rehabilitation services will thus be noted very soon after the injury.

In summary, then, careful screening of about half of all men who are seriously and permanently disabled on the job should locate the 1 man in 3 of this half who would seem to be in *special need of rehabilitation,* if he is not to become a permanent "unemployable." Altogether, this process will locate about 4 in 5 of all men who ultimately turn out to be in the "very poor or no" job category. We cannot guarantee that these "poor employment prospects," if offered rehabilitation, will necessarily take it and become well employed and self-supporting; we can only point out that these are the men who seem to be most in need of rehabilitation. Furthermore, since hardly 1 man in 10 in our study had received any vocational rehabilitation or training, we can only infer that those most in need of vocation rehabilitation are not the ones receiving it.

OTHERS WHO MIGHT BENEFIT FROM VOCATIONAL REHABILITATION

The men whom we just examined were the job failures—the men who, some five years after the accident which brought them into our study, were in the "very poor or no" job category. These are the men who seem to be in special need of rehabilitation—rehabilitation which they never received.

Now let us turn our attention to the partially successful group, those whom we have designated as in the "same or somewhat poorer" job category. Although these men had worked the full year prior to the interview (in 1960), their earnings were the same or less than they had been at the time of the accident. Since wages in the New York Metropolitan Area had gone up significantly during the latter part of the 1950s and this group of men had not received increases, we may ask: has their injury left them in a deteriorated employment condition which could have been corrected by proper vocational rehabilitation?

We know only that very few of these men, about 1 in 10, had received any job training whatsoever following injury. How many may have been offered vocational rehabilitation we have no way of knowing. We know only that many of them were earning less than at the time of injury and therefore had probably not returned to a fully productive and satisfying pattern of living.

Can our indicators select out such men who, although they may not be in special need of rehabilitation, could have benefited from it? The answer is: many such men can be picked out by the indicators previously presented. Half of all the men in the "same or somewhat poorer" job group fall into one or more of these categories: 1) all men with chain injuries, 2) of remaining, those who did not return to work for same firm as of time of accident, 3) of remaining, those aged 45 and over who had eight years or less of schooling.

Altogether then, this selection process would designate a little over half of all the men in the study. Of this group, about 1 man in 3 would be in serious need of vocational rehabilitation and another one would probably be able to use it to advantage.

87

Part III

JOB TRAINING, JOB ADJUSTMENTS, AND JOB SEEKING

[8]

Job Training

Each of the workmen's compensation systems with jurisdiction over the men in our study makes some kind of provision for vocational rehabilitation of men injured on the job. Since funds are available for maintenance while undertaking this rehabilitation, it is rather surprising to find only 1 man in 7 (14 per cent) answering "yes" to the question: "Since your injury (illness) have you learned any new skills or trades?" (Possible probes: Go to school? Take a rehabilitation program? Take any courses?). As our net was cast pretty wide, it is probable that this proportion was a good deal higher than it would have been had we insisted on a more organized, structured kind of training as, for example, formally returning to school, undertaking a formal rehabilitation program, or becoming apprenticed under a formal program. Hence, small as it was, the proportion answering "yes" can be taken as the maximum with such job-related training (Chart 8-1).

The reasons offered for a negative answer to this question were quite diverse. Most of the men said that they did not need to learn anything new, that they were able to return to their former jobs, that they could do the same things they had done before. There were others, however, who said they could not afford the money or the time or who said they did not want to, or did not think they were fit for anything. Still others thought they would be unable to get a job, no matter what they did.

We saw previously that about 1 man in 5 was in the group of "very poor or no" jobs; these are the men who failed to make a satisfactory job adjustment, and presumably were most in need of vocational rehabilitation. How many of these men may have been in such poor physical condition as to make rehabilitation extremely difficult? Our data cannot provide a precise answer to this question. We can only point out that very few men reported that they "cannot work at all"—between 4 and 5 per cent of all the men studied. These men who claimed that they "cannot work at all" were all in the group of "very poor or no" jobs, and constituted one-quarter of this labor performance group. Indeed, the large majority of those with "very poor or no" jobs responded to our questions in such a way as to suggest that physical limitations did not preclude the possibility of vocational rehabilitation.

Among the men who failed to make a satisfactory labor market adjustment (most of whom were not employed at the time of interview), only 1 man in 10 claimed to have learned a new skill or trade, or to have undertaken any additional schooling. For all practical purposes this proportion is the same as that for all the men in the study.

Chart 8-1.   PER CENT OF MEN WHO LEARNED NEW SKILLS*

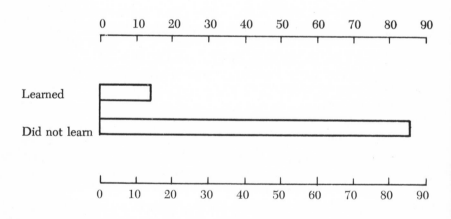

* Based on answers to question: "Since your injury have you learned any new skills or trades?"

92

What was learned by those men who did acquire a new skill or trade, or who received additional schooling, was highly diverse. It ranged from the use of an artificial limb to the acquisition of handicraft skills. More of them learned clerical procedures than anything else; yet the proportion doing so was about 13 per cent of the small number who acquired any new skill. About 1 in 9 learned to repair machinery or appliances and an equal proportion acquired some more formal schooling.

The vocational and retraining sources were also widely variable. Most men (60 per cent) went to a school of some sort, where they learned such diverse things as clerical skills, machine operation, and photography. Sixteen per cent received on-the-job training, while the experience of others ranged from self-teaching to the completion of a correspondence course in repairing refrigerators. Only 9 per cent of all who learned something new claimed to have learned it at a rehabilitation center.

In short, either the average disabled worker in our study succeeded in selling what skills he had (possibly with a slight adjustment in his job—as we shall see in the next chapter), or he ended up employed at substantially lower wages, or he was not employed at all. Few undertook any additional training in an effort to improve their employment opportunities.

A comparable situation seems to be taking shape in various economically depressed areas of this country and also in cases of extensive technological unemployment. Officials are finding considerable reluctance on the part of the chronically unemployed, or those who face long-term unemployment because of automation, to avail themselves of the opportunities afforded them for retraining designed to make them more employable.[1] As in other characteristics reported earlier, it appears, once again, that the men in our study are little different from the general run of workers in this country who have, for one reason or another, been forced into the ranks of the unemployed.

---

[1] See, e.g., *Progress Report, Automation Committee* (Formed under agreements of September 1, 1959, between Armour and Company and United Packinghouse Food and Allied Workers, AFL-CIO, and Amalgamated Meat Cutters and Butcher Workmen of North America, AFL-CIO), June 19, 1961, pp. 6-7. Also, *New York Times,* December 29, 1961, "Response is Slow in Job Retraining," in which the retraining program in West Virginia is described.

[9]

Refitting the Job to the Disability

Considering the fact that the men studied had been seriously and permanently disabled, and noting all the emphasis in the rehabilitation literature on selective placement, we considered the topic of fitting the man to the job to be highly relevant. But since a complete and thorough analysis of selective placement was outside the scope of this study, we limited our investigation largely to ascertaining how—if at all—the job was adjusted for those men who returned to. the same occupation following injury. Thus our information is about the first job the disabled man worked at immediately following his injury. We have no information on how any subsequent job might have been tailored to fit his physical needs.

For men whose first job following injury was in a different occupation (as compared to the occupation held at the time of injury), we simply tried to ascertain how well the respondents thought the new occupation fitted their physical needs following injury.

RETURNING TO THE SAME OCCUPATION

About 6 men in 10 returned to the same job and occupation, immediately following injury, that they had held at the time of injury. In reply to the question: "Was this job different in any way from the job you had before you were injured?" over half of these men reported that no adjustments had been made in their jobs. Our data tell us nothing about whether job adjustments should have been made in order to improve the suitability of the job to the man. But it is sufficient for present purposes to note that men who returned to the same occupation immediately following their injury had found satisfactory positions in the labor market five years later (see Chapter 6). Accordingly, those men who reported no job adjustments were probably able to function sufficiently well in the unchanged jobs.

Among the men who reported job adjustments, the large majority— 7 in 10—indicated that the adjustment consisted of "less work," either in terms of physical energy or hours worked. Included here were men who replied that the adjusted job requires: "less physical effort," "less work to do," "a smaller number of hours per day or week," and "less night work or overtime work to do."

The remaining 3 men in 10 gave a scattering of answers. About 1 in 8 (of all those reporting job adjustments) said that he now "uses new methods" such as sitting instead of standing, or having a machine adjusted to fit his disability. A very few reported that they had been reduced in rank, given a position affording fewer contacts with other people, or moved to a more accessible part of the building, etc.

Significantly, there were really no differences between the kinds of adjustments made for white-collar workers and those made for craftsmen or operatives and laborers. In all occupational groups, when job adjustments were made they were largely of the "less work" variety.

Nor did it make any difference, so far as job adjustments were concerned, whether the man resumed his same occupation for his former firm or found employment with a different firm. In both cases over half the men reported no job adjustments; and of those who did say that their jobs had been altered in any way the large majority reported "less work."

ENTERING A DIFFERENT OCCUPATION

As we have already noted (Chapter 6), the large majority of men who changed occupations after their injury tended to do poorly in the labor market in the following years. (A few were very successful, of course.) Accordingly, in an effort to determine how well they thought they were adjusted to these new jobs, let us examine the responses of those men who returned to work in different occupations.

The first question asked of these men was: "Do you think that the job you got after your injury was suitable for a person with the kinds of jobs and experience you have had?" Six in 10 reported that the job was "suitable." Does this mean that a proper job adjustment had been made for them? To probe further, we asked a second question: "Did your injury handicap you in any way on the first job you got after you were injured?" Over half replied "yes," their injury had handicapped them on the job, which implies a poor adjustment between man and job.

Altogether only 1 man in 4 of those who changed occupations replied in such a manner as to suggest that he was properly adjusted to his new job, i.e., he replied that the new job was suitable and that his disability had not handicapped him. On the other hand, 3 men in 10 seemed to have been completely unadjusted to their new occupations; they replied that the job was not suitable and that their disability had handicapped them in job performance. We infer that these latter were most in need of vocational rehabilitation.

Clearly, the disabled man who was well adjusted to his new occupation—the first job following his injury—was more likely to have a reasonably successful career in the long run than was the man who was not well adjusted to it. This is indicated by the wide disparity between the two groups in average weekly earnings at the time of interview:

Men who reported that new job was suitable
and injury was no handicap .... $94 weekly wages (median)
Men who reported that new job was not suitable
and injury was a handicap .... $71 weekly wages (median)

The remaining men—those who reported that the new job was suitable but that their injury handicapped them, and those who reported that the new job was not suitable but that the injury did not handicap them— had intermediate average weekly earnings.

At the time of injury both groups were earning substantially the same wages; accordingly, we infer that the nature of the job adjustment immediately following injury was a highly relevant indicator of labor market satisfaction in the future.

[10]

Some Factors in Returning to Work for the Same Firm

We saw in Chapter 6 that the future employment experiences of the disabled man were closely tied in with whether or not he returned to work for his former firm. If he did return to work for the same firm, his subsequent employment history tended to be much better than if he did not. Accordingly, that period following his recovery when the man first attempts to return to work is, for all practical purposes, a period of job seeking.

Of course, some men were assured at the time of their injury that they could return to work for the same firm, either at their former job or at some different job, whichever would seem more appropriate in the light of their impairment. For these men we can say that no real job "seeking" was involved. For the majority of the men, however, the first contact with their firms following their injury seemed to have at least some of the characteristics of a job-seeking interview. Accordingly, in this chapter let us examine some of the factors associated with returning to work for the same firm. For those who succeeded, their job-seeking activities were over, at least for the time being. For those who did not succeed, or did not want to return to the same firm, further job seeking was necessary. These activities are described in Chapter 11.

Here we are directing our attention at the question: why are some men rehired by their former firm and others not? For purposes of study these elements can be separated into two groups: those having to do

99

with the worker and his characteristics, and those having to do with the firm. Furthermore, as we shall see, we can also subdivide these two groups—the workers and the firms—with regard to voluntary and involuntary action on their parts.

Obviously, we should like to disentangle the "cause-and-effect" relationships in this hiring situation. What "causes" a firm to rehire an injured worker? What "causes" an injured worker to leave one firm for another? With the information available to us we can only observe relationships between hiring or not hiring, and the various characteristics of the worker and of the firm. We shall explore whatever insights into "cause and effect" can be gleaned from such relationships. But only further research, extended far beyond the scope of this study, could begin to uncover the relevant causal connections.

PERSONAL CHARACTERISTICS OF THE WORKER AT TIME OF INJURY

Ethnic group. We know from our preceding analysis that Puerto Ricans and non-whites were much less likely to be employed, and, if employed, that they were much less likely to have better jobs than at the time they were injured (see Chapter 4). We know that this was true, also, of those with less schooling and, to a lesser extent, of persons with various other personal characteristics. What, then, about returning to work for the same firm? Does this follow along the same lines?

Certainly it does as far as ethnic group is concerned. Separating English-speaking whites from all other (the latter including English-speaking Puerto Ricans), we find that the former were more likely to have returned to work and, among those who did return to work, more likely to have returned to the same firm—67 per cent versus 57 per cent (Chart 10-1).

Education. There was a tendency for those with less education to find employment with a different firm when they first returned to work following the disability injury. Of all men who had completed eight grades or fewer, about 6 men in 10 went back to work for the same firm, while among the men with more education this proportion was about 7 in 10 (Chart 10-1). Whether personnel men deliberately selected the better educated, or whether other selective factors were operating, we do not know.

Just as those with more schooling (nine grades and over) were more likely to go back to the same firm, so also were they more likely than

100

Chart 10-1. SELECTED CHARACTERISTICS* OF WORKERS WHO RETURNED TO WORK FOR SAME FIRM

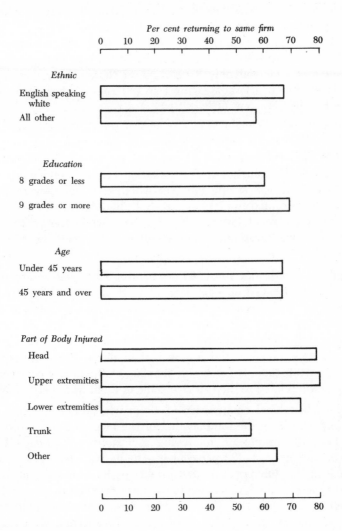

* As of time of injury.

101

those with less schooling to have improved their jobs by the time of the interview. This was true regardless of whether they returned to work with the same or a different firm. Yet, even in this group with more schooling, returning to the same firm was associated with a greater likelihood of job improvement: 53 per cent of those who returned to the same firm were in "better" jobs, as against 44 per cent of those who went to a different one; and only 8 per cent of those who returned to the same firm suffered a loss, as against 16 per cent of those who went to work for a different one (Chart 10-2).

Among those with eight grades or less of school, the relationship was somewhat different. A higher proportion of these men went to different firms (40 per cent as against 31 per cent for those with nine or more years of school); and a higher proportion of them ended up with a lower paying or less steady job. Yet whether or not they returned to the same firm seemed to make relatively little difference. A fifth of them in either employment group suffered a loss, while the proportion experiencing a gain was only slightly different between the two groups (Chart 10-2).

Of all the men in our study, 48 per cent of those who returned to the same firm experienced an improvement in their jobs, while only 32 per cent of those who did not return to the same firm were able to do this. We have seen above that those men with less schooling were less likely to return to the same firm; and that within each of the two categories, men with less schooling did less well than those with more schooling. To what extent, then, is the better showing of the men who returned to the same firm related to the fact that some of them were better educated?

If the educational composition of those who failed to return to the same firm had been the same as that of the men who did return to the same firm, the proportion improving their jobs would have been 40 per cent instead of the 32 per cent it actually was. Hence we conclude that half of the difference in labor market position subsequent to injury, between those men who returned to the same firm and those who did not, was associated with the different educational composition of the two groups. Returning to the same firm was still associated with improving one's job, but so also was having nine or more years of schooling; and personnel men were found to be more likely to rehire a man with more schooling.

Chart 10-2. QUALITY OF JOB HELD AT TIME OF INTERVIEW AND AMOUNT OF SCHOOLING, FOR MEN WHO DID, OR DID NOT, RETURN TO WORK FOR SAME FIRM

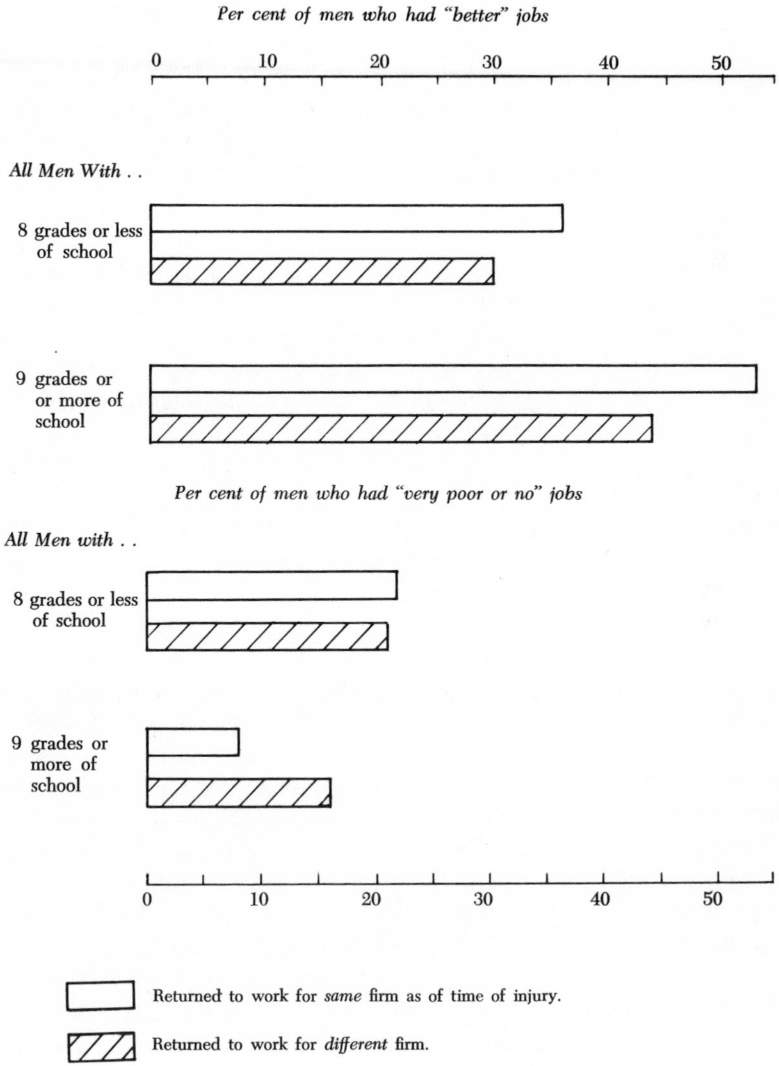

Per cent of men who had "better" jobs
0
10
20
30
40
50
All Men With . .
8 grades or less of school
9 grades or or more of school
Per cent of men who had "very poor or no" jobs
All Men with . .
8 grades or less of school
9 grades or more of school
0
10
20
30
40
50
Returned to work for same firm as of time of injury.
Returned to work for different firm.

Age. There was no difference between our two age groups (under 45, and 45 and over) in the proportion returning to the same firm. But returning to the same firm was much more importantly associated with job improvement among the older group than among the younger. In fact, the younger men were as likely to improve their jobs with a different firm as with the same firm; but among the older men, those who failed to return to the same firm were only half as likely to have improved their jobs by the time of the interview as were those who had been rehired.

Part of body injured. When it comes to the location of injury we find a major departure from our earlier relationships. Though men with injuries to the lower extremities fared less well than others with respect to wage increases and job mobility, they were nevertheless among those more likely to have returned to the same employer (Chart 10-1). The group least likely to have been rehired by the same firm were the men with trunk injuries—back, cardiac, and hernia cases. Yet as far as economic adjustment is concerned, we have already seen that men with trunk injuries did about as well as any other group. It would seem that we have here either a case of prejudice against the hiring (or re-hiring) of persons known to have trunk injuries, or else a situation in which those who suffer such injuries work for companies that have few jobs other than ones requiring considerable physical exertion. The implied result is that once a man is no longer in good physical condition, he has to charge firms in order to change occupations. Also, many trunk (and especially back) injuries may occur to workers who have neither training nor experience beyond simple manual labor. Without retraining, the existence of clerical openings or other less physically taxing work at their previous place of employment would be of small benefit. Surely our data on the relationship between changing jobs and changing occupations give some support to these latter possibilities; but as we shall presently see, there is some support for the former as well. It is also possible that men with trunk injuries—possibly foreseeing the chronic nature of such disabilities—voluntarily sought a different kind of job in order to get lighter work, more suitable working conditions, and so forth.

Since chain injuries so often involve the trunk, we should expect men with such injuries to be rehired less often than men without them. And this is, in fact, what we find. We separated our men into three groups on the basis of their histories of injury as of the time they first returned to work. These were: (a) those who had had chain injuries; (b) those who had not had chain injuries (whether or not later injuries altered the situation), but had suffered two or more injuries; and (c) those who had suffered one injury only. Thus, our categories were based on the information that any personnel officer—or the worker himself—could have had about the latter's history of injury.

There was a substantial difference between those with chains and those without them in the proportions never returning to work. Nearly a third (29 per cent) of the men who had already been found to have chain injuries failed to go back to work at all, while the proportion not doing so among the others was only minimal (6 per cent for those with multiple injuries; 2 per cent for those with only one). But among the men who did return to work, those with chains were as likely as those without them to be rehired by their former firms.

Just why such a high proportion of the men with trunk injuries should never return to work we cannot say. It is possible that one factor was the operation of a kind of "curbstone medicine": the man with, say, a back or heart injury expected it to become worse, and because of this expectation determined to avoid any job in which he might have to put undue strain upon that portion of his body.[1] But workers are not the only ones likely to make a "curbstone" diagnosis. Our few interviews with personnel officers (see pp. 110-112 of this chapter) clearly suggest the operation of such a factor among them, too. With a considerable reluctance on their part to hire men with back injuries (the injury most often associated with a "chain"), it would seem that the firm, too, was an important element leading to the high rate of men with chain injuries who never return to work.

Weekly wages. As we might expect from the close relationship between being a laborer and being in the lowest wage group (under $70 a week), men in this group were much less likely than the others to return to the same firm. Only a little over half of these men returned to the same firm, as contrasted with two-thirds of the men in higher paying jobs.

---

[1] Of course, he might have been right. We know that the number of men whose injuries developed into chains more than doubled between the time of their most serious job-connected injuries and the date of the interview. The number with multiple injuries increased only 17 per cent during the same period. Accordingly, it is entirely possible that many men anticipated the recurrence of an injury and tried to adjust their employment accordingly.

Disabled Workers in the Labor Market

At all wage levels above $70, however, there was but little difference in the proportion rehired by the same firms; it remained at about two-thirds.

Voluntary versus involuntary movers. During the course of our interviews with these men, they were asked why they returned, or did not return to work for the firm in which they were employed at the time of injury. Among the men who subsequently went to work for a different firm, about 4 men in 10 gave an answer indicating that they had voluntarily changed jobs. The remaining 6 either gave indefinite answers or indicated that the firm they had worked for at the time of injury had refused to rehire them.

We saw previously that 29 per cent of the men in our study went to work for a different firm following their injuries. If some 40 per cent of these men changed jobs voluntarily, then we can calculate that about 12 per cent of all the men whom we studied changed jobs voluntarily, and that perhaps 17 per cent did so involuntarily. How do these proportions compare with those on separation rates among workers in general? The materials on manufacturing workers offer some clues.

During the course of a year, 15 to 20 per cent of all U. S. workers in manufacturing voluntarily leave their jobs, while a somewhat higher proportion may be laid off. The specific proportions, of course, depend on the stage of the business cycle. These figures for all persons in manufacturing do not seem to differ greatly from the estimated separation rates which we found among the disabled men in our study. Hence, it seems likely that those factors which motivate workers in general to make voluntary changes in jobs operate also to some extent among men who are disabled.[2] In addition, some may be motivated to change because of their disability, as a result of which they wish to obtain a different type of occupation. The possible relevance to rehabilitation problems of voluntary and involuntary mobility will be discussed subsequently.

Summary. The factors which influenced the worker in returning (or failing to return) to work for his former employer are, in general, about the same factors which influenced his subsequent employment status, his job mobility, and his wages. Ethnic group and schooling were, perhaps,

---

[2] For discussion of factors involved in job changing see, for example, Herbert S. Parnes, *Research on Labor Mobility.* Social Science Research Council, Bulletin 65, 1954, especially Chapters 4 and 5. See also Abraham Bluestone, "Major Studies of Workers' Reasons for Job Choice," *Monthly Labor Review,* V. 78, No. 3, March 1955.

106

somewhat less important here than elsewhere, and wages and occupation at the time of injury perhaps somewhat more. But the general relationships lay in the same direction and had about the same dimensions. The only difference—and it may be an important one from the standpoint of vocational rehabilitation—was the greater likelihood that a person with a trunk injury would not be rehired by his former employer.

CHARACTERISTICS OF THE FIRM

If the characteristics of the individual worker are of some importance in determining his level of employment and—among the disabled—in determining whether he will be rehired by the employer for whom he worked at the time of injury, it is unlikely that they are the sole determinants. For hiring and firing involve firms and personnel officers no less than workers, and all of these factors must operate within the larger social and economic context of which they are a part. It is, then, to some of these factors on the other side of the hiring process that we now turn our attention.

Firms going out of business. Obviously a firm that has gone out of business can no longer employ or re-employ those who used to work for it. We do not know how many of the men in our study were unable to return to their former firms because of this, but we can estimate that very few—perhaps not more than 1 man in 20—was in this predicament. Some of those men formerly employed in construction undoubtedly found the projects on which they had worked completed when they applied for rehiring. Although the firm still continued in business, new projects might not replace those terminated or might be geographically located elsewhere.

Precise information is not available on the number of firms which went out of business in the New York Metropolitan Area during the years in which our men first returned to work following injury. But we can calculate as follows: In New York State a little over 1 per cent of the firms become business failures each year; this is a minimum estimate of the proportion of men under study who were unable to return to their firms. On the other hand, some 7 per cent of all employees in the United States worked in firms which discontinued operations in 1959; this is our maximum estimate of the proportion of our disabled men whose firms went out of business.[3] In short, we conclude that only a small proportion

---

[3] Another 7 or 8 per cent of all employees in the United States work in firms

of the disabled men did not return to work for their former firm because the firm had discontinued business. Other factors were far more important.[4]

Industry. The industry in which a man worked at the time of his injury was quite clearly associated with the likelihood of his returning to the same employer. Those in non-durable goods manufacturing when they were injured were most likely to return (71%); those in durable goods manufacturing were almost as likely (66%). Next was trade (62%), followed by finance and public administration (61%), transportation (60%), construction (55%), and finally service, least likely of all industry groups (54%). (Chart 10-3).

Physical demands upon a worker certainly differ among industries, and account for some part of the differences between industry groups in returning to the same employer. Also, rehiring policies may differ among industries, and the degree of union influence towards rehiring may also differ. But it should also be noted that in such industries as construction, projects might be completed or new ones undertaken in other locales while the injured worker was convalescing, precluding re-employment through simple unavailability of the former job.

Here we have considered returning to the same employer, or not returning, for all persons in our sample, including the approximate 6½ per cent who never returned to work at all following their injury. If these latter persons are excluded, findings are somewhat different.[5]

---

which transfer ownership during a year. If we assume that re-employment is unlikely in a firm which has changed ownership, then we can assume that 15 per cent of the men studied would not be able to return to their former firm because it was no longer there. However, since the majority of the disabled men returned to work within six months of injury, there was only a half year or so of time in which the firm, as of the time of injury, could have gone out of business or transferred ownership. Hence, our maximum estimate of the proportion of our disabled men whose firms went out of business between time of injury and time of first return to work, remains at around 7 or 8 per cent.

[4] Information on business failures from Dun and Bradstreet, Inc., N. Y., *The Failure Record Through 1959,* as published in: United States Bureau of Census, *Statistical Abstract of the United States:* 1961, Washington, D. C., p. 499. Information on firms discontinuing operations from United States Department of Commerce, Office of Business Economics, as published in *Statistical Abstract of the United States:* 1961, p. 480.

[5] If we compare the proportion returning to the same employer, *excluding those who never returned to work,* with the proportion returning to the same employer, *including those who never returned to work,* the industry category with the highest

Chart 10-3. PER CENT OF MEN IN EACH INDUSTRY
WHO RETURNED TO WORK FOR SAME FIRM

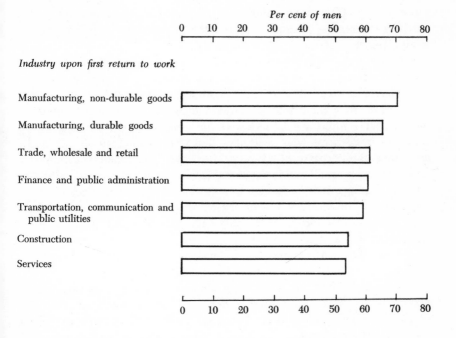

proportion returning shifts from "finance and public administration" to "non-durable goods manufacturing." Federal employees are the great majority of "finance and public administration," and we conclude that these persons tend either to return to former work, or else not to return to work at all.

Per cent returning to the same employer . . .

	. . . excluding "never returned to work"	. . . including "never returned to work"
Non-durable goods manufacturing	72	71
Finance and public administration	75	61

109

Size of firm. Among manufacturing firms, there is a hint that larger firms (those with 100 or more employees) were more likely to rehire their disabled workers than were the smaller firms—79 per cent as against 68 per cent—but the number of firms involved was too small for this difference to be statistically significant.[6] However, it is most significant that the direction of this difference conforms with the findings of the *Survey of Employers' Practices* that "more of the very largest firms (i.e., those having 500 or more employees) reported having knowingly hired partially disabled applicants, than did the intermediate size firms (those having between 200 and 499 workers)."[7]

Attitude of the employer. There is evidence from an earlier study[8] that the attitudes of employers are an important determinant of the rate of employment of physically handicapped workers. In an attempt to ascertain to what extent this was a factor in the re-employment of men in our sample, we interviewed the persons responsible for hiring practices in 23 firms who, we knew, had rehired someone in our study, and their counterparts in 21 other firms we knew had not done so. Although such small numbers of cases cannot supply statistically significant findings, it is important to note that all the differences between the two sets of answers lay in the same direction. Negative answers (i.e., against the hiring of a physically handicapped person) were more common among those who had not rehired than among those who had, both with respect to the hiring of new employees and the rehiring of an old employee who had been injured.

With respect to the four different kinds of handicaps we asked them about, there were substantial differences within each of the two employer groups, as well as between them. Both groups expressed the greatest unwillingness to hire a person with a back injury, and the least unwillingness to hire a person who was blind in one eye. Though persons with heart ailments or orthopedic handicaps were far more undesirable than those with blindness in one eye, opposition

---

[6] Information on size of firm was obtained by looking up the names of the firms for which our respondents stated that they had been working at the time of their injury in the *Industrial Directory of New York State*, State of New York, Department of Commerce, 1958; and in *New Jersey Industrial Directory*, New York, New Jersey State Industrial Directory, Inc., 1960-61, and earlier.

[7] Federation Employment and Guidance Service, *Survey of Employers' Practices and Policies in the Hiring of Physically Impaired Workers*, N. Y., 1959, p. 20.

[8] *Ibid.*

110

to hiring them was not as great as to hiring persons with back injuries, as shown in the following figures:

Per cent personnel men expressing opposition to hiring
persons with specified handicaps, and who in fact . . .

Specified handicap	. . . did not rehire person in sample	. . . did rehire person in sample
Orthopedic	43	35
Loss of one eye	19	9
Back	62	39
Heart	52	30
Number interviewed	21	23

What a person says about an abstract situation, and what he does in a concrete one, may be quite different things, of course, and not too much can be done with the few interviews we have. But it is interesting to note that those who did not rehire the men in our study were, as a group, more negatively inclined toward physically handicapped workers in general. It is also interesting to note that among both groups of firms, the opposition to men with back injuries was substantial—despite the fact that our data suggest that these men, if employed, do about as well on the average as any other group.

Summary. With respect to the relation between rehiring and the characteristics of firms, we know that a few firms had gone out of business and that government workers were more likely to be rehired than were construction workers. But apart from these observations our data yielded little additional relevant information as to why some firms rehired their disabled employees and others did not.

A small additional set of interviews with personnel men gave support for an earlier research finding that showed the attitudes of personnel men to be an important determinant of hiring policies for the physically handicapped. In general, the personnel men in firms which had rehired disabled employees were somewhat more favorably inclined toward disabled workers. But the interviews were too few to permit conclusions beyond this. We still need more information about individual firms. If a personnel man is more or less reluctant to hire—or rehire—a worker with a particular disability, is it because he has had some experience with that individual or with that type of worker? Is it because of the way he defines the abilities necessary for the kinds of work operations in his firm? Is it just habit—or what?

Moreover, are firms that hire relatively unschooled, unskilled workers more likely to have a rapid turnover of workers? Are they more likely to be marginal employers, and hence more likely to go out of business? To these questions, relevant as they are to the labor market experiences of the disabled worker, our data can give no answers.

[11]

Job Seeking

About half the men in our study went job hunting at some time between their injury and the time of interview. These were the men who either did not return to work for the same firm in which they were employed at the time of injury, or else did return and subsequently left. As of the time of interview, three-quarters of these men were employed, —i.e., their job hunting had been successful. The remaining quarter divided almost equally into two groups: those still seeking jobs and those not looking (as of the time of interview), although many of these latter had previously sought work. Let us examine these three groups separately.

THOSE EMPLOYED AT TIME OF INTERVIEW

The two leading procedures for finding jobs were: applying directly to the firm, and inquiring of friends and relatives. Altogether, 57 per cent of the men reported finding their jobs in one or the other manner. Labor unions found employment for 1 man in 6, and employment offices for 1 man in 9. The few remaining men found their jobs in miscellaneous ways (see Chart 11-1).

The most outstanding observation which we can make is that this pattern closely resembles that of all manual workers, as reported by Parnes.[1]

---

[1] *Op. cit.*, pp. 162-63. Quoted with permission of the Social Science Research Council.

113

"It is apparent that manual workers most often learn about jobs either through friends or relatives, or by direct application at the gate. These methods of finding jobs account for between 50 to 85 percent of the cases. . . . In contrast with these techniques for finding jobs, the more formal methods are surprisingly little used. Although the findings vary, in general the studies show that not more than a tenth of the workers find their jobs through public employment offices, that similarly small proportions learn about jobs through advertisements, and that even fewer find work through private employment agencies or unions. . . . The patterns followed by workers in seeking jobs are apparently rather firmly ingrained. When Reynolds asked a sample of employed manual workers how they would go about finding a job if they were out of work, the responses followed rather closely the pattern of their past behavior."

Chart 11-1. JOB SEEKING TECHNIQUES

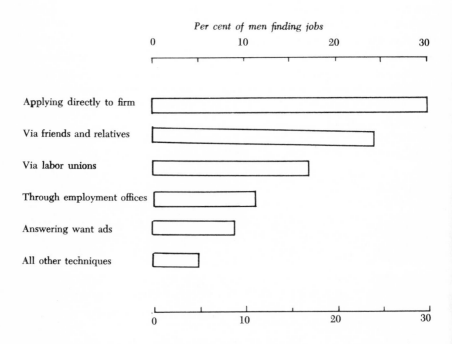

114

Apparently the disabled men made no more use of employment agencies than do the general body of workers, despite the fact that special employment offices with the mission of placing disabled workers exist in the New York Metropolitan Area. Why the workers apparently made so little use of these public and private employment offices we do not know.

THOSE SEEKING WORK AT TIME OF INTERVIEW

Men seeking work at the time of interview reported having used an average of four job-seeking techniques. Most of them had sought work through friends and relatives, some three-quarters had applied directly to firms, and an equal proportion had used want ads. About half reported that they had applied to employment agencies, and one-third that they had tried through labor unions. Only 1 man in 7 reported that he had sought employment through a rehabilitation center.

Presumably, some of these men who were seeking work will succeed in finding it. As of the time of the interview, about 1 in 8 said that he had been promised a job. How many additional men will succeed in their job hunting we do not know; we only know that about one-third of them reported that their "chances of getting a job, compared to others with the same vocation and experience," were "better" or "the same." In short, in addition to the men who said that they had been promised jobs, there were some others who seemed reasonably confident that they too would find work.

THOSE NOT EMPLOYED AND NOT SEEKING WORK

Apart from a few—about 1 in 8—who reported that they had been promised a job, those men who were completely out of the labor force (i.e., neither employed nor looking for work) had apparently made but little effort to find jobs following injury. Not only were they not seeking work at the time of interview, but a number reported no job-seeking activities whatsoever over the entire period since their injuries. Those who had sought jobs at one time or another had used the same techniques previously mentioned: they had applied directly to employers, made use of job agencies and rehabilitation centers to some extent, answered want ads, and sought jobs through friends and relatives. Why so few of these disabled men reported having made use of the existing job agencies which specialize in placing disabled workers, we do not know. None of them gave any indication of being optimistic about finding employment.

Part IV

MEN OUT OF WORK

[12]

The "Hard Core"

We have seen that nearly 1 in 5 of the men in our study had made a poor adjustment to the labor market, i.e., he was in the "very poor or no" job category. This is the group we are referring to as the "hard core"—those men who, in the year prior to the interview, either did not work at all or worked only part time at wages lower than those they were receiving at the time of their injury.

Before proceeding with a description of these men we may ask: Were they, by any chance, marginal workers before their injuries, or were their pre-injury employment histories about the same as those of other men? The answer is that before their injuries, these men were not very different from those men who subsequently made reasonably good adjustments to the labor market. The present "hard core" men compare with the other men as follows (Chart 12-1):

a) somewhat more of the "hard core" group had been operatives and laborers, rather than white-collar workers and craftsmen;

b) because of this lower occupational position they earned a little less (at time of injury); their median weekly earnings were $86 as compared with $96 for all other men;

c) the "hard core" men had experienced appreciably more accidents or illnesses prior to the workmen's compensation injury which brought them into our study;

d) in the three years prior to their workmen's compensation injury, the "hard core" men had worked almost as consistently as the other men; about 3 in 4 of the "hard core" men had been out of employment for less than one month in these three years.

119

Chart 12-1. SELECTED CHARACTERISTICS FOR "HARD CORE" AND OTHER MEN, AS OF TIME OF INJURY

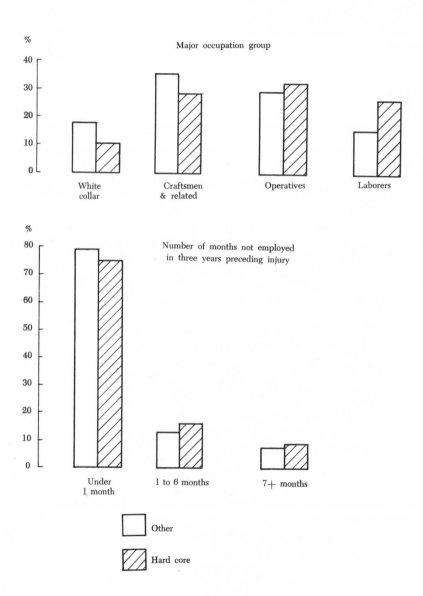

Now, since the "hard core" men had pre-injury employment histories which were not very different from those of other men, and since none of the "hard core" men had yet (in 1960) reached the age when most workers in this country retire from the labor force, it follows that their poor showing in the labor market, as of the 12-month period preceding the interview, was in some way related to their having been injured on the job. And furthermore, since by definition all the other workers in our study had made a reasonably satisfactory adjustment to the conditions of the labor market, it seems fair to conclude that this "hard core" group of disabled workers was, of all the men in our study, the one most in need of vocational and, perhaps, non-vocational rehabilitation.

As we have already seen how these men compare on a variety of characteristics with the rest of the men in our study (Chapters 4 and 5), we shall not repeat that set of comparisons here. Instead, we shall attempt in this chapter a more detailed description of these men, in the hope of giving those most concerned with the provision of vocational rehabilitation and related services a useful summary of the main characteristics of these injured workers.

THE TYPICAL MEMBER OF THE "HARD CORE" GROUP

Here we shall characterize the typical "hard core" man in our sample. In statistical terms this is the modal "hard core" man, who may not necessarily resemble in all particulars those at the furthest extremes of employment failure. This modal man will, however, be most typical of all men in the generally unsuccessful "hard core"—men in the "very poor or no" job category. In turn, then, he represents the numerical majority of those with pressing need for assistance, and his typical characteristics should, in considerable measure, determine or modify the form of that assistance.

The typical member of this group was, at the time of his most serious job-connected injury, an operative earning between $80 and $89 a week. He was a non-Puerto Rican white and possessed of no more than a grammar school education. Between injury and interview, this modal person underwent no additional schooling, no training program, no rehabilitation, except the medical care demanded by his injury or illness. At the time of the interview he was at least 45 years of age, not employed, living in a four-person household, with a total family income during the preceding 12 months of between $3,000 and $4,000. He had suffered more

121

than one injury or illness serious enough to keep him out of work for at least a month,[1] the most serious of which he received in either 1956 or 1957; and he complained of both physical and emotional problems. He visited with friends more than once a month.

PERSONAL CHARACTERISTICS

These men tended to be in the older ages, 45-59. Less than a third were under age 45. (Chart 12-2).

A high proportion (28 per cent) were Negroes, Puerto Ricans, or Orientals.

Most (77 per cent) were married and living with their wives.

Very few lived alone, while almost half lived in households of four or more persons.

So far as schooling is concerned, they tended to be concentrated in the lower levels; more than half had eight years or less. Nevertheless, 1 out of 12 had completed at least one year of college, and nearly a third had completed at least the eleventh grade. Schooling was very highly related to age: 6 out of 10 of the older men had failed to go beyond the eighth grade, whereas for the younger men this ratio was but 3 out of 10. There was not much difference in education between the whites (excluding the Puerto Ricans) and other ethnic groups.

ECONOMIC CHARACTERISTICS AT THE TIME OF MOST SERIOUS JOB-CONNECTED INJURY

Nine out of 10 of these men were manual workers at the time of injury. Only 11 per cent were white-collar workers. A third had been operatives, while slightly less than a third had been in each of the other two categories: craftsmen, and service workers and laborers (Chart 12-2).

Their median wage at the time of injury was $86. In general, the operatives had the lowest wages and the craftsmen the highest. More than three-fifths of the latter had weekly wages of at least $90, whereas only slightly more than a fourth of the operatives were at this wage level.

ECONOMIC CHARACTERISTICS AT THE TIME OF INTERVIEW

In the year preceding the interview (an average of five years following the most serious job-connected injury), only 37 per cent of these men were employed, and then only part time. Of these, 15 per cent were

---

[1] Or otherwise seriously modify or alter his customary work routine.

Chart 12-2. CHARACTERISTICS OF DISABLED MEN WHO MADE POOR ADJUSTMENTS TO THE LABOR MARKET FOLLOWING INJURY

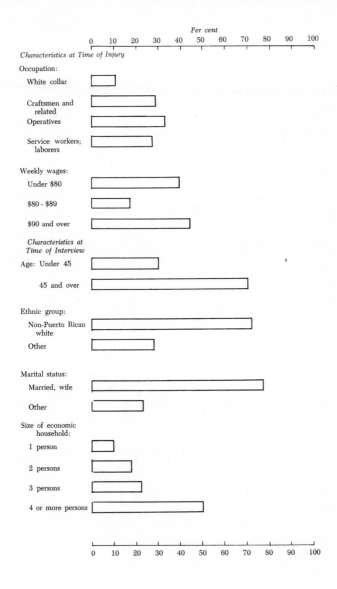

Chart 12-2 (continued). CHARACTERISTICS OF DISABLED MEN WHO MADE POOR ADJUSTMENTS TO THE LABOR MARKET FOLLOWING INJURY

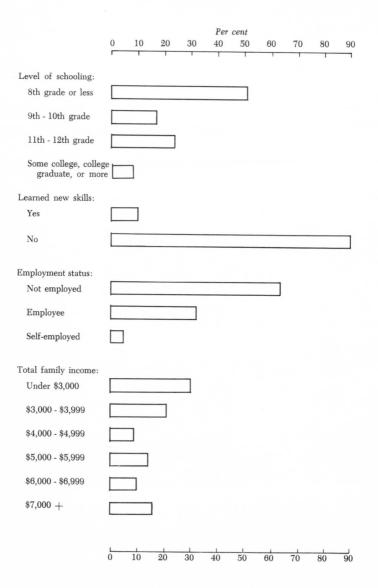

self-employed. The number employed as white-collar workers had not changed; but the number employed as operatives was only one-sixth of what it had been at the time of injury. The decline in the number working as craftsmen was nearly as great, while the number employed as laborers or service workers was down most of all.

The median wage of the few men who were employed was $77 a week—a drop of $9 from that for the whole group at the time of injury, and this despite a general increase in wage levels in metropolitan New York during this five-year period. More than 4 out of 10 had a wage of less than $70. Only slightly more than a third had a wage of at least $90.

The total family incomes of these men were similarly concentrated in the lower categories. Over half had less than $4,000 in the year preceding the interview; only a fourth had $6,000 or over. The incomes of the younger men tended to be slightly higher, though the difference was too little to be significant.

Only 10 per cent of these men had learned a new skill or trade, or acquired additional schooling since injury. This is a smaller proportion than that of the "same or somewhat poorer" job category (12 per cent had learned something new) or of the "better" job category (17 per cent had done so).

JOB OUTLOOK

As a group, these men were decidedly pessimistic about their future job opportunities. Of those not employed at the time of the interview, 3 out of 4 thought their chances of getting a job were inferior to the chances of other workers with the same experience and skills. Only 1 out of 20 thought they were any better. Fourteen per cent of these non-employed men said either that they had a job promised to them or expected to be employed soon. What is significant here is that this was such a low proportion of the total. It would seem that possibly as many as 20 per cent, or as few as 5 per cent, of the non-employed among these men were likely to get jobs of some sort in the future.

THE MOST SERIOUS JOB-CONNECTED INJURY

Over half of these men received their most serious job-connected injury in the period, 1954-1956. A fifth received it as late as 1957, while over a fourth did so in 1953 or earlier.

More than a third had trunk injuries of various kinds: back, heart,

125

hernia. A fourth suffered internal injuries, or injuries to multiple parts or locations of the body concurrently.

As could be expected from this high incidence of trunk, internal, and multiple part or location injuries (i.e., multiple so far as the location of the most serious job-connected injury is concerned), the proportion of these men with chain injuries (40 per cent) was quite high. The proportion who had been injured more than once among those without chain injuries was about the same as for the study as a whole. But altogether, fewer than a third of these men had only one non-chain injury.

MOST RECENT INJURY

A substantially larger proportion of these "hard core" men than among the fully employed men received their most recent injury no longer ago than 1957. This we would expect in view of the high incidence of chain injuries among men in this classification. Nevertheless, it is probable that some of these men were still in the process of recuperation at the time of the interview and could, therefore, be expected eventually to return to work, assuming they had no further "links" in their chains. We cannot pinpoint any specific number, however. We have just noted (Chapter 11) that a small proportion of these men reported that they had been promised jobs, or expected to be employed soon. Maybe this is the group recovering from recent injuries. It may also be the group which, in its own opinion, or that of the employer, or both, appears quite likely to recover fully, without undue likelihood of recurrence of a physical problem.

PHYSICAL AND EMOTIONAL CHARACTERISTICS

The overwhelming majority (87 per cent) of these men reported either physical or emotional problems at the time of interview (Chart 12-3). Six out of 10 mentioned having *both* kinds of problems. There was little difference between the two age groups (under 45, and 45 and over) in this respect. The older men were somewhat more likely to mention physical difficulties, while the younger were more likely to mention emotional ones. The distribution of mentions was essentially the same in both ethnic groupings, too. It was the same again in the various categories locating injuries—except that men with injuries to their lower extremities were less likely to mention *both* physical and emotional problems.

Not surprisingly, men whose most recent injury occurred in 1958 or later were about half again as likely to have problem mentions as were those whose most recent injury occcurred before that date. In fact,

126

Chart 12-3. PHYSICAL AND EMOTIONAL ATTRIBUTES OF DISABLED MEN WHO MADE POOR ADJUSTMENTS TO THE LABOR MARKET FOLLOWING INJURY

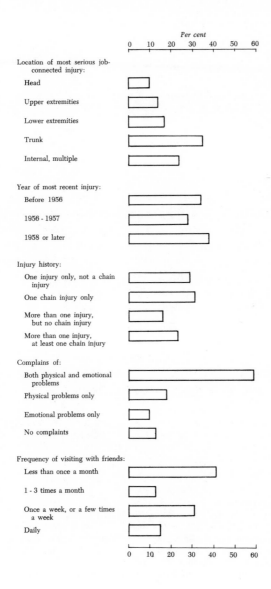

every one of the men in the more recent injury category (an injury in 1958, 1959, or 1960) reported a problem; 70 per cent reported both physical and emotional problems, 30 per cent physical problems alone. No one in this group mentioned only emotional problems.

Men with chain injuries were somewhat more likely to have problem mentions and considerably more likely to have both kinds—physical and emotional.

The distribution of mentions by number of years of schooling revealed that men at all educational levels reported physical and emotional problems.

"Hard core" men who were married and living with their wives, and "hard core" men of other marital status, all mentioned physical and emotional problems.

Another clue to the emotional state of these "hard core" men can be found in the degree to which they got together with friends. This can be an important variable in rehabilitation, for it suggests the difficulties in reaching these men and the extent to which they are likely to take— or be emotionally or physically able to take—an active role in any program of rehabilitation. The proportion who visited friends less than once a month was higher among these "hard core" men than among either of the other two labor performance groups (see Chart 12-4).[2] It may be a source of some optimism, as far as rehabilitation is concerned, that two-thirds of this proportion of the men said they would like to see friends more often than they did. But the fact remains that whether or not they *said* they wanted to see friends more often, these men *did not actually see* them at all often. We suggest that what they *do*, rather than what they

---

[2] A question similar to the one used in our study was asked in 1945 of a cross section of Minnesota men age 30-59, with the following results:

Less than once a month	9%
1 to 3 times a month	11
Once a week or more	80
	100%

Though possibly due in part to the fact of disablility among the men in our study, the differences may be attributed in part also to the fact that all of the men in our study lived in a metropolitan area of several million population, while none of the Minnesota sample lived in an area of one million population and only a fourth lived in a metropolitan area of 250,000 or over. (The Roper Public Opinion Research Center at Williams College, Williamstown, Mass. kindly furnished us this Minnesota data, obtained in The Minnesota Poll, sponsored by the *Minneapolis Star and Tribune*.)

Chart 12-4. FREQUENCY OF GETTING TOGETHER WITH FRIENDS

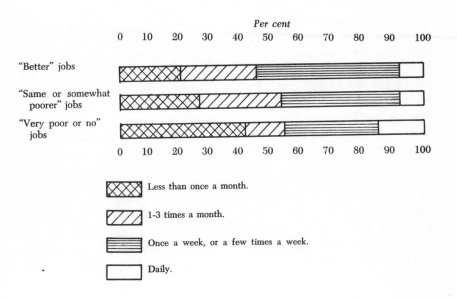

say they would like to do, is the more important indicator for rehabiliation programs. The importance of friends as sources of "job leads" is quite relevant here.

USE OF WELFARE AND RELATED AGENCY SERVICES

We have already seen that, in terms of wages and employment histories during the three years preceding the most serious job-connected injury, the men in this "hard core" group were only a little different from the rest of the men in our study. Nevertheless, we did not want to reject the possibility that what we had in this group were representatives of a permanent "hard core" element in our society: persons who show up frequently on relief rolls; persons who often receive assistance from family counselling agencies; and so forth. Accordingly, we made arrangements with the Community Council of Greater New York, Inc., to check their Social Service Exchange[3] for information on either these men themselves or members of their immediate families to see whether they had made use of the services of any welfare or health agencies.

We did not ask for a search on each of the men in this group. We felt our needs could be met by information on a comparative few: 25 selected at random from those who had made a poor adjustment and 30 from those who had made a satisfactory one. The results were quite definite: the "hard core" men and their families were far more likely to need (or at least use) various kinds of assistance than the men who had made a good adjustment to the labor market following injury. Unfortunately, our interview data did not include important information used to identify a man on the index such as his wife's maiden name, which would distinguish one person from another with the same name at the same address. Therefore, a number of "poor adjustment" persons and one "good adjustment" person were not conclusively identified as users. Of the eight men in the "poor adjustment" group who had used the services of one or another agency, one had used services of the New York Office of Vocational Rehabilitation, one had put a child out for care in a foster home, and six had been on public welfare at one time or another (one of whom had also made use of the Domestic Relations Court).

---

[3] A cooperative activity of public and voluntary welfare and health agencies, the Social Service Exchange maintains a central index of persons who have been known to one or more social agencies. It thereby (1) assists agencies in determining responsibility before accepting clients or making definite plans for their care or treatment; (2) facilitates mutual planning among social workers on behalf of clients; (3) promotes greater coordination of effort among agencies; and (4) enables social agencies to avoid duplication and overlapping of services for clients. The master file contains information on about two and a half million persons who have used the services of about 300 social and health agencies with some 700 separate units among them.

130

	Poor adjustment	Good adjustment
Not listed at all	2	26
Identified as a user of services of at least one agency	8	1
Member of a family identified as user of services of at least one agency, but not himself a user	2	2
Not conclusively identified, although probably a user, or a member of a using family	12	1
Out of area covered by Index	1	0
Total Class Searched:	**25**	**30**

However, there is no conclusive evidence that this is a "permanent hard core" group. It should hardly surprise us that a man seriously injured on the job happened to make use of the state's vocational rehabilitation program. The surprise, in fact, is that the number who did make use of this service should have been so small. In the case of only two individuals can we be sure that the use of agency services was made *before* they became disabled. Also, in no instance was a person recorded as making steady use of one or another form of assistance (including welfare). If the report of agency contacts is an adequate indicator, they appeared to go on welfare and then get off it again. Only one had been on welfare during 1961, for instance. Finally, we should recall that before injury these "hard core" men had worked fairly steadily and had earned average wages. On the other hand, we should also remember that the Index has been expanding its agency coverage over the past ten years, and is undoubtedly receiving fuller data today than in earlier years. Also, as in any such reporting, not all relevant agency usage is reported since not all agencies in the area cooperate, and inevitably there are omissions in the reporting of those that do cooperate.

It is possible that our "poor adjustment" group is neither a "permanent hard core" nor simply a "post-injury hard core." Rather, they may be persons, or members of families, which manage to surmount normal problems, but lack physical, emotional, economic, or vocational resources adequate for a traumatic occurrence such as a serious injury or illness. If such is the case, they might be termed a "permanent high risk" group.

[13]

Means of Support When Out of Work Because of Disability

We have already seen that almost all of the men in our study were married and living with their families, and as such were primary earners. We have also noted (Chapter 1) that workmen's compensation payments could have amounted to hardly half of the earnings of these men prior to injury. While median weekly earnings at the time of injury were about $90, the maximum weekly awards payable were only $30 or $40 (depending on the year of injury) in New Jersey; $36 in New York; $35 or $54 (depending on the year of injury) for longshoremen and harbor workers coming under Federal jurisdiction. For Federal employees, however, the maximum award was $121. Clearly, only the Federal awards were high enough not to force the disabled worker to suffer a sharp decrease in family income. But since Federal employees were such a small proportion of the total, the effect of this higher maximum on the total distribution of awards to the men in our study was negligible.

Since these awards were so low relative to earnings, and since nearly every one of the men in our study was out of work for at least some time as a consequence of his injury, an important question concerning the adjustment of these men to their disabilities was the following: "Would you mind telling me how you and your family supported yourselves while you were out of work?"

Most of the men received support from more than one source. All together, they reported an average of 3.4 sources apiece. The distribution of these sources follows:

133

Disabled Workers in the Labor Market

	Per cent of total[a]
1. Personal sources	86
Used savings	63
Borrowed money	40
Received help from friends or relatives	39
Sold or pawned something	16
Other family member went to work	15
2. Social insurance sources	88
Received workmen's compensation	84[b]
Received sickness or disability benefits	17
Received Veterans Administration benefits	9
Received unemployment insurance	7
Member of family received Social Security	2
3. Public welfare	5
4. Lost no pay	6
5. Other[c]	36

[a] Percentages add to more than 100 because of proportion who received support from two or more sources.

[b] Some men collected the major part of their workmen's compensation benefits after returning to work.

[c] Includes other member of household already working, and miscellaneous sources not elsewhere specified.

Virtually everyone in our study relied on one or more of the following sources: borrowing money; help from friends or relatives, or the earnings of other family members; savings; workmen's compensation; or disability benefits. Of the 94 per cent in our study who lost some pay during the period following injury, a mere 5 per cent became public charges. Disablement threw men out of work (for the most part, only temporarily, as we have already seen), and it reduced family incomes. But it did not result in much addition to the relief rolls. (Chart 13-1).

This is similar to the findings on a group of unemployed workers in Albany, Schenectady, and Troy, New York, in the spring of 1957.[1] There

---

[1] *Benefits, Incomes and Expenditures of Unemployed Workers*, Report of a Survey Conducted by the Bureau of Applied Social Research, Columbia University, for the State of New York, N. Y., New York State Department of Labor, Division of Employment, September, 1958, Tables 13 and 14, pp. 50-51.

134

Chart 13-1. SOURCES OF SUPPORT WHILE OUT OF WORK FOLLOWING INJURYa

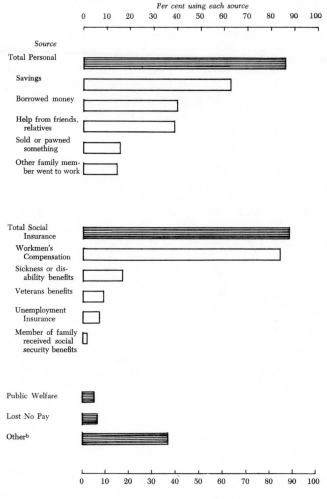

a Sources total more than 100% because multiple mentions were possible in answer to this question.

b Includes other member of household already working, and miscellaneous sources not elsewhere specified.

135

the proportion going on relief during their period out of work was also only 5 per cent. As with the men in our study, the unemployed in the Albany area used their savings, borrowed money, obtained help from friends and relatives. They also postponed purchases (particularly of medical and dental care) and dropped insurance coverages.

Family size. Apart from another member's going to work or remaining in employment—possibilities which were, by definition, unavailable to those men in single-person families—there was little difference by family size in the proportion engaging in the various types of financial adjustment. Each family size group was about as likely as the others to borrow money, use savings, or send another member of the family to work.

Nor was there any difference by family size in the number of different sources utilized, despite the fact that one might expect the larger family to have a greater variety of supports available to it. The average number utilized by single person families was 3.3, by two and three person families 3.4, and by four or more person families 3.5.

Numbers of major sources used. Dividing the sources of support into three major types—personal, social insurance, and public welfare—we find that about three-fourths of the men in our study made use of two sources during the time they were out of work following injury. For all but a handful, these two were social insurance (i.e., workmen's compensation) and personal (savings, borrowings, employment of other family member, etc.). Fourteen per cent used but one source, with the number about evenly divided between social insurance and personal sources. About 4 per cent made use of all three types, and 6 per cent lost no wages while not working. There was no significant difference by family size in any of these proportions. Significantly, there was not a single family entirely dependent on public welfare.

APPENDIXES

APPENDIX A

METHODOLOGY

DEFINING THE UNIVERSE

The characteristics of the universe were determined on the basis of: (a) the purpose of the study, and (b) the nature of the data available for selecting persons to be interviewed. Each was important as a limitation on the other.

It was decided to exclude women from our study, first, because so few are injured on the job, and second, because their experiences in the labor market are generally so different from those of men. It was decided also to confine our study to men who would be no older than 59 at the time of interview. This we did partly to eliminate any bias resulting from the greater difficulty for markedly older workers in seeking re-employment once they have been out of work for a while, and partly because we wanted to focus our attention on persons who would, in the normal course of events, have at least several years of employment ahead of them.

A further limitation resulted from the area covered. This we restricted to the New York Metropolitan Region, consisting for our purposes of the five boroughs of New York City, Nassau and Westchester Counties, and the western part of Suffolk County in New York State; and the northwestern New Jersey counties of Bergen, Essex, Hudson, and Union, together with that eastern tip of Passaic County which includes the cities of Passaic, Paterson, and Clifton. There were two reasons for thus confining ourselves. One was to achieve a kind of standardization for general economic conditions, since this area presumably

139

constitutes more or less of a single labor market. The other was to minimize enumeration costs in both money and time.

Since our emphasis was to be on employment histories, *subsequent* to recovery and re-entry into the labor force, we wanted to obtain interviews only from men who had time to recover about as much as they were ever likely to, and who had also had time to get back into the labor force. Yet we also wanted to obtain viable addresses in a number large enough to be representative of the universe. The more remote the date of injury, the less viable the address was likely to be. After discussing the matter with our medical advisor and with personnel in the various workmen's compensation jurisdictions, the following compromises were reached:

From the New Jersey jurisdiction we selected cases closed (i.e., adjudicated) in 1956 and 1958 (excluding those involving injuries occurring after September 30, 1957). Most of these involved on-the-job injuries occurring within the two years preceding the date of closing. Of all the New Jersey universe, 55 per cent came from cases closed in 1956, the remaining 45 per cent from cases closed in 1958.

From the New York jurisdiction we selected our cases from among those closed in 1957. The majority of these involved injuries which had occurred within the three years preceding the date of closing.

With respect to Federal cases, our method of selection differed somewhat because of different administrative procedures in these programs, and also because of the relatively small number of workers involved. We finally settled on those injured any time between January 1, 1950 and September 30, 1957. Because of the presumed difficulties of interviewing them, we excluded longshoremen, a precaution which seems to have been unnecessary in view of the success we had contacting and interviewing the few longshoremen in our universe who came under either of the other two jurisdictions.

Our universe, then, was comprised of all men:

    a) under 60 years of age in 1959,
    b) recipient of workmen's compensation for serious, permanent disablements (except for longshoremen covered under the Federal system),
    c) resident in New York Metropolitan Area at the time of the disablement and still resident there at the time of interview,

140

d) not involved in any workmen's compensation or third-party litigation at the time of interview, and

e) whose cases were adjudicated in 1957 (for New York) or 1956 or 1958 (for New Jersey, excepting those injured later than September 30, 1957). For men covered by the Federal program (Federal employees and those on temporary duty with the Federal Government, e.g., members of the military reserve on active duty, together with shipyard and drydock workers) the timing was on the basis of the date of injury, since our universe was limited to men injured any time between January 1, 1950 and September 30, 1957.

The respective workmen's compensation boards decided whether or not a person was "permanently impaired." The criteria for *"seriously impaired"* were arrived at as follows: on the advice of our medical consultant we decided to make the criterion of minimum severity equal to the total loss of a thumb; this entitles a worker to 75 weeks' compensation in each of the three jurisdictions. It is a serious disability. On the basis of the schedules of awards it is equivalent to a loss of about 25 per cent of the use of a hand, or 36 per cent of the use of a foot.

The task of selecting the seriously impaired from the New Jersey cases was relatively easy because under that state's program every permanent disablement is, for all practical purposes, a *scheduled* injury (i.e., a determination is made of the degree of incapacity and the beneficiary given payments for the number of weeks stipulated in the schedule for that extent of disability). Moreover, in New Jersey the maximum amount of compensation which the beneficiary could receive was so low that nearly every worker qualified for it. Accordingly, we defined the New Jersey part of our universe, so far as disability was concerned, as including all workers who had received workmen's compensation of at least $2,250 (for cases closed in 1956) or $2,800 (for cases closed in 1958, when the maximum was higher) for permanent disablements suffered on the job.

The New York cases presented a more difficult task of selection on the basis of severity. The scheduled disabilities were easily selected. But about half of the New York cases were non-scheduled; compensation for them was determined, instead, on the basis of lost earnings. This group included injuries to back, shoulder, or neck, and cardiac and occupational diseases. No matter how serious his non-scheduled disability, if the victim suffered no loss of income as a result, he received no compensation under the New York system.

141

However, most of the men with non-scheduled permanent disabilities did experience some loss of income. And over the years the amount of money many of them received amounted to more than that received by the seriously disabled person with a *scheduled* disability. For these reasons it was decided to include in our universe *all* of the men with permanent, non-scheduled disabilities who were awarded compensation because of lost earnings, or for whom a determination of "lost earning capacity" was made. A few others with permanent, non-scheduled disabilities who suffered no loss of income, and hence received no compensation, were added; a review of their records by our medical advisor showed them to be disabled seriously enough to qualify.

It should be noted that men with non-scheduled, permanent disabilities who received no award had, by definition, suffered no loss in earnings. Therefore, they must have continued in employment at the same, or higher, earnings. If these cases had been omitted our universe would have been slightly biased toward the unemployed or loss-of-income group. This was the major reason for including them.

Another group initially added to the New York portion of our universe was made up of persons who had received serious, permanent facial disfigurement. Since only 10 per cent of all such cases received $500 or more, it was felt that this sum would be a suitable minimum for inclusion in our universe. This turned out to be far too low, however, since many of these "serious, permanent" disfigurements were all but imperceptible to the interviewers. We retained some of these cases for our universe, those few who reported substantial current physical limitations when interviewed; but most (some 66 in all) had to be discarded from the analysis because their disfigurements were so slight as hardly to constitute a potential block to current or past employment.

The Federal selection was made in much the same way as the New York selection, except that with most of these we could refer to the full case record, medical report and all, in reaching a decision.

In short, we made every possible effort to make the cases from each of the three jurisdictions conform to the same criteria. But as might be expected, complete comparability is impossible when working with materials collected in different jurisdictions and in accordance with different laws and different definitions.

RESPONDENTS WHO SUPPLIED LIMITED INFORMATION

Not everyone who answered our letter, or with whom we made contact by telephone or personal visit, consented to be interviewed. We did find, however, that from all of them (or from a member of the household) we were able to elicit information on current labor force status (i.e., whether employed, unemployed, looking for work, or out of the labor force) and, in most instances, on occupation and industry, if employed at time of interview. This was of considerable importance in view of the labor market orientation of our study.

SUBSEQUENT CHANGES MADE IN DEFINITION OF THE UNIVERSE

We have already noted that 66 New York cases with facial injuries were removed from our universe because their injuries were found to be very minor. These 66 cases were persons who consented to the full interview. An additional 50 New York cases, persons from whom we obtained only the few items of employment data, were also removed. This was in line with the more rigid criteria for seriousness which we felt obliged to adopt after our experience with the first 66. Thirteen others (4 New York, 8 New Jersey, and 1 Federal) were also removed from the full interview sample because, upon being interviewed, they were found to indicate no current limitations whatsoever.

Since our interview approached the physical state of the respondent in many ways, in detail and at length, we feel that it has considerable reliability. We can only assume that injured persons may sometimes escape, at a later date, the unfavorable prognostic categories in which they were placed when injured.

SOURCES OF DATA

The New York State Workmen's Compensation Board supplied us with the name and last known address of each man who met our criteria for inclusion in the universe, together with whatever characteristics of the person would be useful for sampling purposes.

We selected the New Jersey cases ourselves from duplicates made of the IBM jurisdiction cards for all cases in 1956 and 1958. The identification numbers were then used to obtain names and last known addresses.

With Federal cases the procedure was somewhat different. The administration procedures for persons still receiving compensation differ

143

from those for persons who no longer do. The former we obtained by going through the case records of each of these men (the records are all housed in the New York office of the Bureau of Employees' Compensation). Those not now receiving compensation were selected according to our criteria by the Division of Research of the Federal Bureau of Employees' Compensation, Chambersburg, Pennsylvania. For some, the Division was able to supply names and addresses. For the rest, it made arrangements for the case folders to be sent to the New York office where we could inspect them directly.

Our sources of data, then, were of two types: interviews and official case records. From the latter we were able to get a wealth of information on such matters as age, occupation and industry, and wages at the time of accident; also amount of award, location and nature of injury, severity of injury, and (for New York) cause of injury. We could not from this source obtain information on such important matters as labor market experience, present physical condition (at the time of our interview), other injuries and illnesses, and job changes. For information on these and other topics dealing with the periods preceding and following injury, we had to rely on personal interviews. The considerable information made available to us from official records, however, did mean that on a number of important variables the characteristics of our universe were known. This made it possible not only to make a number of analyses of the entire universe (the calculation of injury rate tables, Appendix D, for instance), but also to determine just how representative of the universe was the group we finally succeeded in interviewing.

CONSTRUCTION OF THE INTERVIEW QUESTIONNAIRE

Probably no social survey questionnaire is made out of whole cloth. There are some questions—on age, marital status, schooling, for example—which appear to be common to all. For our own survey we were able to borrow and adapt a number of questions, particularly on labor force status, from the United States Census Current Population Survey. Others we obtained from an earlier survey, conducted by the Bureau of Applied Social Research, of unemployment insurance recipients in Albany and Utica, New York. The advantage of borrowing is that these questions had already been pre-tested—and on a comparable population. Unfortunately, however, only a fraction of the questions we used on the questionnaire could be obtained from these sources. Hence, it was still necessary for us to do considerable pre-testing.

There were, all together, some 150 pre-test interviews during the various stages of questionnaire construction. The majority of these were with persons undergoing rehabilitation at the Institute for Crippled and Disabled, New York City. Others came from the Kessler Institute, West Orange, New Jersey; the Newark Branch of the New Jersey State Employment Office; and the special training program for the aged operated by the Federation Employment and Guidance Service, New York City.

The pre-test interviews were not altogether adequate. Certain questions, particularly those on the characteristics of the present job, could not be asked because none of the pre-test interviewees were employed. Others—those pertaining to workmen's compensation, for instance—could be asked of only a very few. Upon interviewing the universe, we found still other instances in which our pre-test had, for one reason or another, failed to reveal certain shortcomings in the schedule. This was particularly true of the questions on the labor force experience of other family members, the respondent's ability to use certain forms of transportation, and in the whole area of related and unrelated disablements (i.e., "chains," "episodes," and "links"). Fortunately, most of these revealed themselves soon enough for us to make the necessary adjustments in the questionnaire before too much time and money had been wasted.

THE INTERVIEWERS

Forty-two different persons were engaged at some time in the interviewing: 36 men and 6 women. However, only 18 of the men and 4 of the women did 20 or more interviews. These interviewers were a somewhat heterogeneous group so far as age, schooling, occupation, and experience are concerned. For instance, 4 of them were professional survey research interviewers; 6 were interviewers for the New Jersey State Employment Service; one was a pharmacist, one an optician, one an insurance salesman, and one a case-worker for the New York City Department of Welfare. Three had their Ph.D.'s in sociology; two were actors (one of whom was also a playwright); one was a high school teacher, another a lawyer, and another a draftsman. The rest were graduate students.

Among them, they had a speaking knowledge of some five foreign

145

languages, of which only three—Spanish, Polish, and Italian—were ever needed during the course of the interviewing.

All had completed the equivalent of high school, but 10 had not completed the equivalent of college. The oldest was in his 60's, the youngest just 21. Most were in their late 20's and early 30's.

The possibility of adding to their incomes surely attracted some of the interviewers, although our rates were lower than those offered by commercial organizations. But from what many of them told us during the course of the field work, it appears that the prestige of doing research for Columbia University and the personal satisfaction gained from the knowledge that our findings might help people were also strong attractions.

TRAINING THE INTERVIEWERS

Each interviewer received seven to eight paid hours of training before going into the field. The training sessions consisted of reading and discussing thoroughly the written instructions for each question, listening to a tape recording of a mock interview, and then participating in a mock interview. In some cases it was possible for the trainee interviewer to sit in on an actual interview before being turned loose on his own.

The interview schedules were edited as soon as possible after completion. If there were any errors, the schedule was returned to the interviewer for correction. In this way our editor was able to point out to each interviewer the places where he was making mistakes. On occasion, certain interviewers were brought back to the Bureau for supplementary training. In general, it was felt that, by reducing interview errors, these supplementary sessions saved much more time and money than they cost, in addition to furnishing us with more reliable information on our respondents.

CONTACTING THE RESPONDENTS

We used three different techniques of contacting respondents: letters, telephone calls, and (for a very few) personal visits. The initial attempt was made by mail. This varied a bit over time, but those who did not respond were sent at least three letters. The first was printed on a Columbia University letterhead and offered a brief explanation of the project, together with information on how to arrange for an interview (see Exhibit A). Attached to it was a reprint of a brief article on the project that appeared in the New York *World Telegram and Sun* (see Exhibit B). If this elicited no response within about three weeks, we sent out another letter, also on Columbia stationery, which offered a bit more detail on the project, and we hoped, made a stronger appeal for cooperation.

Later on, we were able to send another mailing which included a copy of Mrs. Eleanor Roosevelt's column, "My Day" (see Exhibit C), in which she described the project and its purposes, together with a letter she wrote (see Exhibit D) on her own letterhead, urging the respondents to cooperate. Not everyone was convinced however; but, by and large, the Roosevelt mailings evoked quite a favorable response. As one respondent said, "I got those other letters and did not think much more about it, but when I got the letter from Mrs. Roosevelt, I *knew* it must be pretty important, so I called right away." Others enclosed notes addressed to Mrs. Roosevelt, apologizing for not answering the earlier letters.

In quite a number of instances, the respondents answered with a request for more information, or with the statement that they did not have the time, or that they were all right now. We answered each of these with a personal letter—some 50 in all—and succeeded in getting interviews with about two-thirds of them, and information on current labor force status from nearly all the others.

Many still did not answer, however. In an attempt to get these, we turned to the telephone. By a careful search through directories for every part of our study area we were able to make contact with quite a sizable proportion of those who had not answered our letters. Of the many we found who had moved, quite a number claimed not to have received any of our mailings. Some we were able to talk into being interviewed, while from nearly all the others we obtained information at least on current status in the labor force.

Our first mailings went out third class, not to save the small difference in postage but because, for this class of mail, the law requires the post office to notify the sender of any change in address. This was only moderately successful. We did receive some information from the post office, but later investigation on our part turned up so many cases in which a letter should have been returned to us when, in fact, it was not (e.g., when the building had been torn down) that we were forced to conclude that as many as a third of those who failed to respond were actually per-

147

sons who never received our mailing or were no longer in the universe because they had moved out of the study area.

But there was another, more important reason for abandoning this class of mail. Just as its name implies, third class mail is not always delivered promptly. We found instances of delays in excess of three weeks. Moreover, it often receives rough handling. The combination of these postal problems with the fact that third class mail did not seem to be providing us with enough information on changes of address prompted us to abandon third class mail in favor of first class. This speeded things up considerably and made it easier to introduce a new and even more time-saving way of contacting respondents—a telephone call if they had not answered within ten days.

As the interviewing progressed, it became obvious that we were not likely to get interviews with a large enough proportion of the low wage, low occupation group. Since many of these had no telephone, we decided to try to contact them directly by calling on them at home. To do this we first located their residences on a map of the study area and then sent an interviewer out to those areas where there was a cluster of three or more potential respondents. We often obtained more than one interview and additional future appointments in a single trip. But for the most part we found only that the addresses we had for these men were no longer correct. Sometimes the new tenants or neighbors could give us a more recent address, but usually they could not or would not. In several instances, we found that the building—or even the whole block of buildings—had been torn down.

LOCATION OF INTERVIEWS

Respondents were offered a choice of being interviewed at home or coming to Columbia University at our expense. A surprisingly large number (10 per cent) chose the latter. Some had the idea that, despite our disclaimers, this was actually a job interview. Others seemed to want to check for themselves on the legitimacy of our activity, while still others apparently just wanted a change from their daily routines. Whatever the reasons, their doing this saved us interviewing costs and time.

REMUNERATION OF FIELD WORKERS AND RESPONDENTS

The amount paid those who elected to come to the University for their interview was usually only thirty cents for the subway, but sometimes it was the cost of a train ride from out on Long Island, or bridge tolls and a parking fee. We did not pay car mileage, nor did we pay the respondent anything for his time. We did, however, try to reimburse him for telephone calls, and also gave him enough for a cup of coffee if the interview lasted through a coffee break.

Interviewers were paid by the hour for all the time spent working on the project—that is, for time spent in training, actual interviewing, transportation, editing, making corrections, and arranging for interview appointments. We preferred to risk paying a bit more this way than to pay by the interview and risk getting a sloppy job from a person trying to hurry through it. The pay for interviewers was $1.50 an hour for the first 20 interviews and $1.75 an hour thereafter. In addition, interviewers were reimbursed for all telephone calls, postage, subway and bus fares, tolls, etc., and for car mileage at the rate of nine cents a mile.

COSTS OF FIELD WORK

The total amount spent on field work was $22,321. This excludes the amount spent for pre-testing and for salaries of the regular staff. A more detailed list of the expenditures follows:

Payroll Expenses	$ *Amount*	*Time (in hours)*
Training of interviewers	734	458
Interviewing (incl. transportation time)	7176	4616
Telephoning (to schedule interviews, get answers to questions on current labor force status, etc.)	2740	1825
Coding	1704	1030
Clerical (at Columbia University)	1936	1319
Clerical (New Jersey)	543	402
Clerical (New York)	480	—a
Sub-Total:	**15,313**	**9,650**
Other Expenses	$ *Amount*	
Interviewers' expenses (travel, postage, etc.)	2495	
Travel by staff	449	
Telephone (outside Columbia University)	504	
Telephone (at Columbia University)	517	
Paper (estimated)	500	
Printing	493	
Postage	1125	
Other	925	
Sub-Total:	**7,008**	
Total:	**22,321**	

a Non-ascertainable.

149

Disabled Workers in the Labor Market

PROPORTION OF THE UNIVERSE CONTACTED

Since our universe was limited to those with the specified characteristics who were still living in the New York Metropolitan Area at the time we sought to interview them, it was necessary to estimate for each age group the number who had died and the number who had moved out of the area during the period between date of injury and 1960 (the year during which virtually all the interviewing took place).

For convenience, it was assumed that in the average case the duration of this period was five years. It was also assumed that the 1958 United States life table survivor rates for all males would provide a useful approximation of the number surviving long enough to be interviewed. Applying these rates[1] to the age distribution in the re-defined universe in each jurisdiction (i.e., the universe after the elimination of those currently in litigation, or with minor facial injuries and/or no current limitation), we estimated a loss through death of 27 to those in the New York jurisdiction, 24 in the New Jersey jurisdiction, and 11 in the Federal.

The adjustment for losses due to out-migration was more important because of its magnitude and the considerable differentials by age. It was also more complicated. We used the migration rates for the one-year period, April 1958-April 1959, for the total United States.[2] We assumed that the age relationships in New York would be the same as those in the whole country, and that the proportion in each age group moving out of New York during the five-year period, 1955-60, would be approximately two and one-half times the proportion of those the same age in the whole country who changed their county of residence during the one-year period, April 1958-April 1959. This calculation yielded an estimated loss through out-migration of 253 in the New York jurisdiction, 191 in the New Jersey, and 55 in the Federal. These calculations, together with estimates of the proportion of those in the actual universe whom we either succeeded in interviewing or obtaining current labor force status for, are presented in Table A.1.

It can be seen that subtraction of out-migrants, deaths, litigation cases, and minor injuries reduces considerably the size of our universe: 2,328

---

[1] *Vital Statistics of the United States, 1958,* Section 5, "Life Tables," Table 5-B.

[2] Bureau of the Census, *Current Population Reports,* Series P-20, No. 104, September 30, 1960, Table 4, p. 13.

150

from an original 3,298, a reduction of nearly 30 per cent. Of this latter universe we were able either to interview, or obtain labor force information on, a total of 1,316 (56.5 per cent). Only 21 (lower than 1 per cent) refused outright to give us any information.

That still leaves a large number unaccounted for. But of these we know that 744 (32.0 per cent) were never contacted. All letters addressed to these men were returned, and we were unable to reach them through either the telephone or a personal visit. We have no way of knowing how many others we failed to contact from among those for whom the letters were *not* returned. We know from our experience with several mailings on this study that letters failing to reach the person to whom they are addressed are not invariably returned to the sender. In an attempt to get some idea concerning the proportion of the universe we succeeded in contacting and interviewing, we established minimum and maximum percentages on the basis of two opposite assumptions: (1) all deaths and out-migrants were *included* within that number we know we failed to make contact with (this would *maximize* the figure for the number contacted); and (2) all deaths and out-migrants were *not* included within that number we know we failed to make contact with (this would *minimize* the figure for the number contacted). With the range thus established, we can say with reasonable assurance that we managed to interview, or obtain labor force status on, no fewer than 61.4 per cent and no more than 83.1 per cent of those in our universe whom we succeeded in contacting. The limits were virtually the same for both New York and New Jersey, but a bit higher for the Federal cases, reflecting the larger proportion in the upper ages in that jurisdiction (and suggesting, possibly, that our estimate for the proportion leaving the area was a bit too low—which, if true, would mean that our minimum and maximum figures were also too low).

In addition to the deceased and the out-migrants, an unknown, but probably small, number of institutionalized persons were not contacted, or else were too ill to respond. We did interview a few individuals in hospitals. In several instances our letters were returned from hospitals with notes explaining that the addressee had been discharged. Further efforts to locate the individual failed. We conducted a small number of interviews with persons seriously ill, or handicapped in particular ways such as to make an interview extremely difficult. Here relatives assisted in supplying factual data, and in clarifying unclear responses. As in all

151

Table A.1.

ORIGINAL UNIVERSE, RE-DEFINED UNIVERSE, AND POPULATION ENUMERATED

	N.Y.	N.J.	Federal	Total
1. No. with whom contact was originally attempted	1778	1119	401	3298
2. No. interviewed: a) Retained in universe	410	325	142	877
b) Removed from universe[1]	70	8	1	79
3. No. for whom only information on current labor force status was obtained:				
a) Retained in universe	190	182	67	439
b) Removed from universe[1]	50	0	0	50
4. Others with but minor facial disabilities	226	0	0	226
5. Removed from universe because found to be in litigation	35	9	10	54
6. Re-defined universe (line 1 − sum of lines 2b, 3b, 4, and 5)	1397	1102	390	2889
7. Est. no. deaths occurring over period to persons in line 6	27	25	11	63
8. Est. no. persons in line 6 moving out of area	253	192	55	500
9. Probable actual universe (line 6 − sum of lines 7 and 8)	1117	885	324	2326
10. Refused to be interviewed, or to give information on current labor force status	11	7	3	21

11. Persons in re-defined universe known *not* to have been contacted (possibly including some who died or moved out of area)	385	273	86	744
12. RECAPITULATION: a) Probable actual universe [i.e., excluding minor facials, no current limitations (where known), cases in litigation (where known), estimated deaths, estimated out-migrants]				
b) Est. *maximum* no. contacted from probable actual universe, assuming *all* deaths and out-migrants fall within the no. in line 11 [line 6—line 11]	1117	885	324	2326
c) Est. *minimum* no. contacted from probable total universe, assuming *no* deaths or out-migrants fall within the no. in line 11 [line 12a — line 11]	1012	829	304	2145
	732	614	238	1584
13. Interviewed + those for whom we have only labor force status, as a percentage of probable actual universe	% 53.7	% 57.3	% 64.5	% 56.6
14. Interviewed + those for whom we have only labor force status, as a percentage of *maximum* no. contacted from probable actual universe	59.3	61.2	68.7	61.4
15. Interviewed + those for whom we have only labor force status as a percentage of *minimum* no. contacted from probable actual universe	82.0	82.6	87.8	83.1

[1] Minor, non-permanently disabling injuries, primarily slight facial injuries.

153

interview studies, however, our study cannot report on the small proportion of persons so physically or mentally ill as to preclude an interview. Nor can it report on the small proportion in jail. We did interview several persons recently released from jail, and can therefore infer that a few non-responders were in prisons. We do know of one instance of an individual in our sample who was in custody on a murder charge.

REPRESENTATIVENESS OF THE RESPONDENTS

Most survey research studies attempt to discover the characteristics of their universes by means of a knowledge of some portion of the sample. If a sufficient proportion of those in a carefully designed sample are interviewed, it is plausibly maintained that the data obtained will be representative of the universe. If the number interviewed is but a small proportion of the sample, then the question arises as to how representative that number is. Our study had one initial advantage over most studies with respect to ascertaining representativeness. Case record data compiled by the three workmen's compensation jurisdictions afforded us background material on the men in our universe, and permitted us to compare the characteristics of those we interviewed with identical data for the universe. We could, and in fact did, make such comparisons at intervals during the course of the field phase of our study, and placed emphasis on contacting men with characteristics under-represented by those interviewed to date. Finally, we compared the characteristics of our total respondents with the characteristics of the universe from which the men were drawn.

From jurisdiction record data we were able to describe our universe by such characteristics as age, occupation, industry, and wages at time of injury; year of injury; and location of injury. All three jurisdictions did not record all of these items, and where this was the case we could only measure representativeness of those interviewed for those jurisdictions that did record an item, rather than for all three jurisdictions combined. Also, for some variables recorded by all three jurisdictions, coding categories used by one jurisdiction were incompatible with those of another, and distributions could not be compared (e.g., industry as coded by New Jersey could not be compared to the New York or Federal data). In general, however, enough valid comparison was possible for us to gain considerable insight into the representativeness of those we interviewed.

Record data, of course, consisted only of items ascertainable up to the date of closing of the case. Subsequent to closing, information on labor force history, medical history, attitudes, mobility, etc., had to be drawn from the interview exclusively. We felt, however, that if the persons interviewed were generally representative of the entire sample universe for major background and socio-economic variables, as well as several variables pertaining to the injury or illness, they also would strongly tend to be representative for those items existing only in the form of interview responses.

Where the existence and form of the available data permitted comparisons between the three jurisdictions combined and our sample, we have presented them in Appendix Table A.2. Where this was not possible, we present comparisons for individual jurisdictions. We compared those whom we interviewed in full with the sample universe, and then made this same comparison for those whom we interviewed in full *plus* those for whom we obtained only items pertaining to current labor force situation. The chi-square test was used to test the goodness of fit.

What do we find when we examine the comparisons? Very briefly, we find that, with the exception of wages, the fit of those interviewed in full to the sample universe is so close that there is a very high probability that the discrepancies may be attributed to chance alone. When we add those who gave us current labor force data only, there are only slight changes in the comparisons, except for year of injury. It appears probable that factors other than chance alone determined, to some extent, whether persons injured in certain years replied to the full interview or only to the current labor force questions. Since our major analysis considers only those fully interviewed, this tendency is not very important.

We obtained data on occupation of the universe at the time of injury only for the men in the New York State jurisdiction. Here lack of fit between those interviewed and the universe is not statistically significant, either for the full interview group or for these persons plus the labor force data group. Laborers, operatives, and service workers are somewhat under-represented, which accords with our field experience that unskilled workers had less stable addresses and fewer phones, and so were more difficult to reach.

Lack of fit was significant statistically for wages at time of injury for both those fully interviewed and those briefly interviewed. The lack of fit exists solely for the New York jurisdiction, but it is sufficient to remain

155

significant for the three jurisdictions combined. It is those on the lower wage levels whom we failed to interview in sufficient numbers, as it was those in the less skilled, and generally less well paid, occupations. We suggest that the explanation is the same for both variables and that, by and large, the under-representation in both cases concerns the same men.

What are the variables for which the interviewed persons do represent the sample universe? They are: age at time of injury (age emerged as of major significance in the analysis); size of award (a measure of level of seriousness of injury, and hence of considerable significance); year of injury; industry at time of injury; cause of injury; location of injury (specifying the "trunk" and "lower extremity" categories which proved of major analytic interest); and finally, occupation for the New York jurisdiction, subject to the qualifications we have already noted.

Our report, then, should be interpreted with the fact in mind that the unskilled and less well paid workers, at time of injury, are somewhat under-represented, although not seriously so, as examination of the percentage distribution shows. Apart from this discrepancy, those interviewed are highly representative of the sample universe on basic socioeconomic and injury variables.

NUMBER OF REPLIES BY LABOR FORCE AND EMPLOYMENT STATUS

In Appendix Table A.3 following, the cross-tabulations of numbers of cases are shown in detail. The reader can see exactly how many men were interviewed in full, for how many we have but partial information, the numbers employed and unemployed, etc.

156

Appendix Table A.2.

COMPARISON OF CHARACTERISTICS OF SAMPLE AND UNIVERSE

Per cent distribution of: (1) entire sample universe,[a] (2) persons interviewed in full, and (3) persons interviewed in full *plus* persons who gave current labor force information

All Jurisdictions Combined; Age at Time of Injury

	Probable actual universe %	Fully interviewed %	Fully interviewed plus current labor force data only %
Under 19 years	2.0	1.9	2.0
20 – 24 years	5.3	5.2	5.6
25 – 29 years	9.6	9.0	9.4
30 – 34 years	14.9	15.3	15.4
35 – 44 years	38.7	39.5	38.3
45 – 49 years	26.2	26.6	26.9
NA	3.3	2.5	2.4
N —	2326	877	1324
X²		P > .98	P > .70

All Jurisdictions Combined; Size of Award

	Redefined universe %	Fully interviewed %	Fully interviewed plus current labor force data only %
Under $2,000*	3.3	3.7	4.2
2,000 – 2,999	17.1	18.7	19.2
3,000 – 3,999	19.3	17.8	18.1
4,000 – 4,999	12.8	11.3	11.6
5,000 – 5,999	10.2	10.3	10.0
6,000 – 6,999	9.2	8.5	8.8
7,000 – 7,999	8.6	8.7	8.5
8,000 – 8,999	7.1	8.8	7.9
9,000 – 9,999	3.5	3.5	3.3
10,000 + over	7.4	6.7	6.3
NA	1.5	2.0	2.1
N —	2850	831	1259
X²		P > .30	P > .10

[a] The entire sample universe differs in size according to various definitions described in the text. Availability of particular items of data precluded using a single definition. The universe used is noted for each variation here presented. Briefly, the "probable actual universe" is a figure based on the number with whom contact was attempted minus cases of minor injuries, non-disabling facial injuries, current litigations, etc., which were uncovered during the field phase of the study. The "redefined universe," in addition, removes estimated numbers of death and out-migrants from the non-responders (bad address, etc.). See Appendix A, table on pp. 152-153, for specific details concerning these categories.

* Persons receiving less than $2,000 were omitted for New York, as it was impossible to equate the universe with the interviewed group on minor facial injury tabulation.

157

Appendix Table A.2.

COMPARISON OF CHARACTERISTICS OF SAMPLE AND UNIVERSE, Continued

	All Jurisdictions Combined; Weekly Wages at Time of Injury				*All Jurisdictions Combined; Year of Most Serious Workmen's Compensation Injury Since 1/1/50*[*]			
	Redefined universe %	*Fully inter-viewed* %	*Fully inter-viewed plus current labor force data only* %			*universe Redefined* %	*Fully inter-viewed* %	*Fully inter-viewed plus current labor force data only* %
Under $50	13.1	9.1	10.0	1950 – '52		12.2	12.1	12.8
50 – 59	11.8	9.8	10.5	1953		7.8	9.6	8.9
60 – 69	17.1	16.1	15.1	1954		14.0	15.2	14.0
70 – 79	15.2	14.9	15.6	1955		26.9	26.0	25.9
80 – 89	13.8	16.9	15.5	1956		27.2	24.5	24.1
90 – 99	8.6	8.7	8.8	1957		11.9	13.2	14.1
100 & over	18.5	22.2	22.1					
NA	1.9	2.3	2.4	NA		0.2	0.1	0.2
N –	2262	724	1065	N –		3294	956	1441
X^2	P > .01		P > .01	X^2			P > .20	P > .02

[*] Including minor facials, no limitations, litigations; it was impossible to remove these from the universe tabulation on this item.

Appendix Table A.2.

COMPARISON OF CHARACTERISTICS OF SAMPLE AND UNIVERSE, Continued

New York Only
Occupation at Time of Injury

	Redefined universe %	Fully interviewed %	Fully interviewed plus current labor force data only %
White Collar	11.5	14.6	15.8
Service	11.5	7.3	6.5
Skilled craftsmen	22.1	31.5	26.2
Operatives	38.9	33.7	36.9
Laborers	16.0	12.9	14.7
NA	—	—	—
N	1397	410	600
X^2		P > .50	P > .70

New York Only
Industry at Time of Injury

	Redefined universe %	Fully interviewed %	Fully interviewed plus current labor force data only %
Const., agr., min.	19.5	19.5	19.2
Trans., util., com.	13.4	12.2	13.2
Trade, fin., ins., real estate	11.0	10.2	11.7
Service	8.0	7.3	6.8
Manufacturing	42.5	45.4	43.7
Public admin.	5.7	5.4	5.5
NA	—	—	—
N	1658	410	600
X^2		P > .80	P > .90

159

Appendix Table A.2.

COMPARISON OF CHARACTERISTICS OF SAMPLE AND UNIVERSE, Continued

160

	Federal Only; Industry at Time of Injury				New York Only; Cause of Injury		
	Redefined universe %	Fully inter-viewed %	Fully inter-viewed plus current labor force data only %		Redefined universe %	Fully inter-viewed %	Fully inter-viewed plus current labor force data only %
Post office	19.0	23.9	23.4	Striking against	3.5	2.7	2.8
Ships, naval	18.3	21.8	17.2	Struck by	22.6	21.2	19.5
Ships, private	44.3	36.6	43.1	Caught, in, on, or bet.	13.2	13.2	11.2
Ars'ls, air bases, etc.	6.2	4.9	4.3	Fall, same level	9.5	11.0	11.0
Other	9.5	9.9	10.0	Fall, diff. level	16.3	18.1	18.4
NA	2.7	2.8	1.9	Slip (not fall) or over-extension (strain, hernia)	25.7	25.1	27.7
				Temperature extreme	3.3	2.4	2.5
				Inhalation, ingest.	2.2	1.5	2.2
				Continuous occupat. activity	.1	.2	.3
				Accident type not elsewhere coded	3.7	4.6	4.5
				NA	—	—	—
N —	400	142	209	N —	1658	410	600
X²		P > .30	P > .50	X²		P > .50	P > .10

Appendix Table A.2.

COMPARISON OF CHARACTERISTICS OF SAMPLE AND UNIVERSE, Continued

	New York Only; Location of Injury		
	Redefined universe %	Fully inter- viewed %	Fully inter- viewed plus current labor force data only %
Eye	4.1	3.4	3.7
Head	4.4	6.8	5.8
Trunk	34.9	34.7	39.2
Hands & fingers	16.2	16.3	13.7
Lower extremities	12.0	14.2	14.3
Mult. body locats., gen., & unclear	9.0	10.5	9.9
Upper extremities	14.4	13.9	13.2
NA	–	–	–
N –	1380*	380*	567
X^2		P almost .10	P > .20

* Excluding all facial injuries.

	New Jersey Only; Location of Injury		
	Redefined universe %	Fully inter- viewed %	Fully inter- viewed plus current labor force data only %
Head, eye, face, neck	4.8	3.7	4.6
Trunk	30.1	33.6	33.7
Upper extremities	7.9	9.5	7.7
Lower extremities	5.4	6.4	5.4
Mult. locations	51.8	46.8	48.6
NA	–	–	–
N –	1108	327	504*
X^2		P > .20	P > .50

* Different from similar sums for different distributions be- cause of: (1) inclusion of two additional interviews and (2) exclusion of five who gave labor status only.

161

Appendix Table A.3.

RELATIONSHIP OF EMPLOYMENT STATUS AND CLASS OF WORKER AT TIME OF INTERVIEW TO LABOR PERFORMANCE GROUP BASED ON LABOR MARKET ACTIVITIES IN YEAR PRECEDING INTERVIEW

Status at time of interview	Class of worker at time of interview			Class of wk. NA
	Self Employed	Employee	Total	
Employed at time of interview	83	661	**744**	392
Preceding year's activities				
Better jobs	29	303	**322**	—
Poorer jobs	35	270	**305**	—
Very poor or no jobs	9	52	**61**	—
NA	10	36	**46**	—
Replied to labor force questionnaires only	—	—	—	392
Not employed at time of interview			**133**	47
Preceding year's activities				
Better jobs			**8**	
Poorer jobs			**11**	
Very poor or no jobs			**103**	
NA			**11**	
Replied to labor force questionnaires only	—	—	—	47
Total	**83**	**661**	**877°**	**439**
Total	**83**	**661**	**877°**	**435**
Preceding year's activities				
Better jobs	29	303	**340**	
Poorer jobs	35	270	**316**	
Very poor or no jobs	9	52	**164**	
NA	10	36	**57**	
Replied to labor force questionnaires only	—	—	—	439
Grand total				**1316**

° Includes men who were not employed at time of interview.

162

APPENDIX B

PREVALENCE OF SERIOUS ON-THE-JOB INJURIES

IN THE UNITED STATES

There were about 4 million men in the United States, 1959-60, between the ages of 17 and 64 who had suffered limitation of major activity sometime during the course of their lifetimes.[1] Of these men about 3-1/3 million reported that they were working at the time the limitation started, about ½ million were not working at the time, and the others were unknown (Appendix Table B.1). "Limitation of major activity" includes those men who replied to the National Health Survey enumerator that they "cannot work at all at present" or "can work but limited in amount or kind."

The rates by age vary from a low of 2.5 per cent for men aged 17 to 24 who reported limitation of major activity, to 19.2 per cent for men aged 55 to 64, to a high of 39 per cent for men aged 65 and over. Most disabled men, with the exception of those in the youngest age group (17 to 24 years), received their limitation while working. Of all men in the United States aged 25 to 54 years, about 5.7 per cent were working at the time the limitation started, i.e., they replied "yes" to the question, "Were you at work at your job or business when the accident happened?" Some 1 per cent were not working at the time. Of men aged 55 to 64 years, over 17 per cent received a limitation while working, and but 1 per cent not while working. Only among men aged 65 and over did a significant

---

[1] Data from unpublished table of the National Health Survey entitled: "Number of Males With Chronic Limitation Affecting Major Activity by Duration of Limitation, According to Employment Status When Limitation Started, Usual Activity Status, and Age: United States, July 1959-60."

163

proportion report that their limitation did not start while they were working. At these older ages the degenerative diseases, of course, play a much more important part in affecting health.

Now let us examine the employment situation of these men subsequent to the time that their limitation of major activity started. Those men who were working at the time the limitation began obviously had work experience. Among these men in the age group 25 to 54 years, about three-quarters were usually working at the time of interview (Appendix Table B.2). That is, during most of the year preceding the interview by the National Health Survey interviewer, they reported that they usually worked at a job. This proportion—three-quarters—is almost the same whether the man had his limitation for less than five years (as of the time of the interview), or for five years or longer. Apparently, if the man was able to return to work, he was able to continue working. Presumably the remaining one-quarter of the men who were not usually working at the time of interview were permanently out of employment; this would certainly seem to be the case for men who had received their limitation at least five years ago.

This proportion of one-quarter is approximately equivalent to the 20 per cent of the men whom we studied and who were found to be in the "very poor or no" job category. Perhaps the labor market experiences of disabled men in the New York Metropolitan Area are not very different from all disabled men in the United States.

Among men aged 55 to 64 years, about half were usually working at the time of interview. Presumably at this older age many men have had more than one incident resulting in a limitation of major activity; furthermore, the degenerative diseases have begun to take their toll. Presumably the combination of these two factors resulted in the observation that about half of the men in this age group were not usually working.

Of the men in retirement age—65 and over—fewer than a fifth were usually working.

It is sometimes thought that people with limitations who have had no work experience find it much more difficult to obtain employment than do those who had work experience prior to the start of the limitation. The available data for young men aged 17 to 24 years tend to support this proposition. Among these youths who were not working at the time the limitation started (most of whom probably had had no work experience whatsoever), about one-third reported that they were usually

164

working as of the time of the interview. However, among men of the same age group who were working at the time the limitation started and who, therefore, had at least some work experience, half were usually working at the time of the interview.

Unfortunately, all of the information needed to test this proposition is not available. We do not know, for example, whether the severity of the limitations was the same for the two groups; it may be that included among those not working at the time the limitation started are many congenital cases so severe that they have never worked and never will.

Examination of the data for the other age groups reveals that in each instance a larger proportion of those who received their limitation while working were reported as usually working at the time of interview (Appendix Table B.2). In these age groups also we do not know whether the severity of injury was the same for the two groups—those who received their limitation while working and those who received their limitation otherwise. We only know that the congenital cases are among the latter group, and some of these people may never have had any work experience at all during their lifetimes.

Next we may ask: what proportion of the employed males in the United States (in 1959-60) were men with limitation of major activity? At ages 17 to 24 years, about 2 per cent had such limitations; at ages 25 to 54 years, about 5 per cent; and among employed men aged 55 to 64 years, perhaps 12 per cent.

Finally, we may compare these findings with the results shown in Appendix E. In this Appendix we shall see that, among men in New York City and in New Jersey, there are about 4 serious job-connected injuries suffered per 100 men between the ages of 20 and 49. This rate is somewhat lower then the rate of 5.7 per cent of all men in the United States (in 1959-60) who reported having a limitation of major activity which started while they were working. We cannot say whether this discrepancy is due to differences in definition of seriousness of injury, to differences between men of the New York Metropolitan Area and men over the entire United States, or to differences in definition between the terms "job connected" and "started while working." We can only conclude that perhaps 1 man in 20 in the United States is so seriously injured on the job sometime during the course of his lifetime as to remain with a permanent limitation of major activity.

Appendix Table B.1.

ESTIMATED NUMBERS OF MEN WITH MAJOR ACTIVITY
LIMITATION BY AGE: UNITED STATES, JULY 1959 - JUNE 1960*

(numbers in thousands)

Age	Total Pop.	Total		Number with limitations				Unknown[a]	
				Working at time limitation started		Not working at time limitation started			
		No.	% of pop.	No.	% of pop.	No.	% of pop.	No.	% of pop.
17 to 24 years	9,200	228	2.5	81	0.9	117	1.3	30	0.3
25 to 54 years	33,000	2248	6.8	1893	5.7	285	0.9	71	0.2
55 to 64 years	7,500	1443	19.2	1307	17.4	78	1.0	58	0.8
17 to 64 years	49,700	3919	7.9	3281	6.6	480	1.0	159	0.3
65 and over	7,500	2947	39.3	2168	28.9	604	8.1	176	2.4

* Source: Unpublished data kindly provided by National Health Survey.

[a] Unknown as to whether man was or was not working at time limitation started.

166

Appendix Table B.2.

ESTIMATED NUMBERS OF MEN WITH MAJOR ACTIVITY LIMITATION BY PRESENT EMPLOYMENT STATUS AND AGE: UNITED STATES, JULY 1959 - JUNE 1960
(numbers in thousands)

	Numbers		Duration of limitation % usually working at time of interview	
	Total	5+ years	Total	5+ years
WORKING AT TIME LIMITATION STARTED				
Age				
17 to 24 years	81	*	49	*
25 to 54 years	1893	871	74	76
55 to 64 years	1307	579	52	55
17 to 64 years	3281	1459	65	68
65 and over	2168	1161	17	14
NOT WORKING AT TIME LIMITATION STARTED				
Age				
17 to 24 years	117	*	35	*
25 to 54 years	285	244	58	61
55 to 64 years	78	*	*	*
17 to 64 years	480	349	43	*
65 and over	604	194	4	*

* Too few cases to show separately.
Source: Unpublished data kindly provided by National Health Survey.

167

APPENDIX C

PROBABILITY OF A SUBSEQUENT SERIOUS INJURY

In the course of the interviews, information was collected about every serious disability, injury, or sickness which the respondent may have had. "Serious" was defined, for our purposes, in terms of an injury which left a permanent disability, or an injury or sick period which resulted in work stoppage for at least one month, or a major job re-adjustment such as a less strenuous job or part-time work. By definition, the workmen's compensation injury which brought the man into our study was a permanently disabling one; of the other injuries and sick periods about which we obtained information, in some three-quarters of the cases the respondent claimed that it had a permanently disabling effect.

We first selected out every man whose first reported injury was the workmen's compensation one which brought the man into our study. We then ascertained the length of time between this injury and the following injury or sick period, if any. This analysis was limited to men whose initial workmen's compensation injury occurred in 1954 or earlier, in order to have a full five-year period following.

Since injuries to the back, traditionally, are supposedly marked by recurrences, we separated the men into the two groups: those whose initial injury was a back injury, and all others. For each group, then, we obtained the number who reported a second injury or sick period within one year, two years, etc. up to five years. Note that the second injury may or may not be related to the first one. It would be desirable that the second injury be to the same part of the body as the initial one, so that recurrence for specific types of injuries could be computed. Because of

168

the small number of cases available, however, we could not calculate such specific injury-recurrence rates.

The probability of second injuries or sick periods within the specified length of time, for the two initial groups—backs and all others—are as follows:

	Initial injury	
Elapsed time	Backs $N = 102$	All other $N = 208$
Within one year	.06	.04
Within two years	.14	.12
Within three years	.25	.16
Within four years	.33	.19
Within five years	.35	.24

At the end of five years, 35 per cent of the men whose initial injury was to the back reported a second injury or sickness, and 65 per cent reported no subsequent injury. Among men whose first injury was to other parts of the body, 24 per cent reported a second injury or sickness within five years time, and 76 per cent reported no subsequent one. Within each time interval, the rates were lower for the "all other" group than for the "backs."[1]

At this point we should ask: how does the probability of a second injury or sick period compare with the probability of a first one? If a man has already had one serious injury, is he thereby more likely to have a second and subsequent one? The literature is saturated with studies which attempt to answer this question, and all are unsuccessful due to the lack of adequate statistics. We have no better statistics than other investigators, but since lack of proper data seems not to disturb researchers, we shall present our estimates of the probability of a man in the general population having a serious accident or injury which prevents him from working for a month or longer.

Let us turn to discharges from hospitals as an index of prevalency of injuries and sicknesses. Presumably, if a man has spent several days in a hospital, he had been quite sick, but not necessarily permanently disabled. During the year July 1957-July 1958, among all men in the United States aged 25 to 44 years, 6.4 per cent were discharged from

---

[1] These differences are statistically significant.

169

hospitals after an average length of stay of 10.9 days.[2] Among men aged 45 to 64 years, 10 per cent were discharged after an average stay of 13.7 days. Presumably, most of these men were sick enough so that they could have been out of work for a month or longer and thereby qualified under our definition of "serious" injury or sickness.

If these rates of discharge from hospitals can be accepted as approximations to the rates of serious injuries and sickness in the general male population, then we can compute that, during a five-year period, on the general order of 32 per cent of males aged 25 to 44, and 50 per cent of males aged 45 to 64, become seriously sick or disabled. Among the men in our study, some 27 per cent had a second injury or sick period within five years following the workmen's compensation incident which brought the man into our study; this includes men of about 25 to 59 years of age. Considering the differences in definition and universe involved in comparing discharges from hospitals over the whole United States with interview data from a group of men in the New York Metropolitan Area, we can only conclude that the men in our study do not seem to be markedly different from all American men. In short, the probability of having a second injury or sick period is perhaps not too different from the probability of having an initial one (after taking into account the age of the men). Undoubtedly there are some exceptions to this, and certain types of disabilities perhaps always have reccurrences; but we have no statistics to refine this analysis any further.

[2] United States National Health Survey, *Health Statistics,* "Hospitalization, United States, July 1957 - June 1958," Series B-7, Table 2; United States Department of Health, Education, and Welfare, Public Health Service.

170

APPENDIX D*

SOME ILLUSTRATIVE RATE TABLES ON
SERIOUSLY DISABLING WORK INJURIES

In the Introduction to this book some general remarks were made concerning disabling injuries and illnesses, both in respect to their prevalence nationally, and to their impact on persons and their lives. In this appendix we are limiting ourselves to one question only: How many job-connected deaths and serious, permanent disablements (in accordance with the definition given in Chapter 1 and Appendix A) will occur by the age of 50 to a cohort of men who began working at age 20 as employees in non-agriculture? (Injury-rate tables of this sort illustrate one type of analysis which can be made from data regularly obtained by state workmen's compensation agencies.)

METHODS AND PROCEDURES[1]

The method followed in deriving our injury-rate tables is essentially that used in computing net reproduction rates. It consists of (1) obtaining the age-specific rates of serious, permanent, job-connected disablement of male workers in any given year, (2) applying these rates to a life table population as a means of standardizing for age and adjusting for

---

* This appendix originally appeared as Exhibit F, "Some Illustrative Rate Tables on Seriously Disabling Work Injuries," by A. J. Jaffe and Lincoln H. Day, in *Research Conference on Workmen's Compensation and Vocational Rehabilitation, 1960*, edited by A. J. Jaffe. New York: Bureau of Applied Social Research, Columbia University, 1961.

[1] Federal employees and certain other numerically minor groups of employees are excluded from the jurisdiction of the New York and New Jersey state workmen's compensation boards. Injuries to such persons are not included in our calculations.

171

mortality, and (3) cumulatively summing the number of these disablements.

Only two kinds of statistics are needed: the age and sex-specific disablements in any given year, and the age and sex distribution of the working population in that year.

The number of disablements and deaths by age was obtained from the workmen's compensation boards. The populations were estimated by interpolation from the Census of 1950, used in conjunction with the 1957 sample Census of New York, and an estimated age and sex distribution for 1955 made by the State of New Jersey. Admittedly, if workmen's compensation data had been available as of a census year, we would have had more precise population data for the denominators since population census tabulations of sex by age by class of worker by industry could then have been obtained.

DISABLEMENTS OVER A WORKING LIFETIME

How many job-connected deaths and serious, permanent disablements (by our definition) will occur by the age of 50 to a cohort of youths who begin working at age 20 as employees in non-agriculture? The number is about 4.1 per 100 such workers in New York City, Westchester and Nassau Counties, and about 3.7 per 100 in New Jersey (see Table D.1.). The rates for permanent disablements only (i.e., excluding deaths) are 3.8 in New York City and 3.4 in the State of New Jersey (see Table D.2.).

The New York rates are higher at nearly every age and in nearly every category for which we have been able to compute them. We do not know for sure why this is. It could result, for instance, from a higher accident rate per industry in New York, or from a difference between New York and New Jersey in the criteria used by the medical examiners, or as a result of the fact that we could not define "permanent disablement" in identically the same way in both states.

What is needed is rates for specific and detailed industries like those we have already calculated for the three major industrial groups (described below). This cannot be done with statistics for only one year, however. Because the number of injuries in individual industries would be so small in any given year, it would probably take a whole decade to obtain enough cases to permit making any reliable calculations for detailed industries (at either the 2 or 3 digit level). Such calculations would furnish extremely important information, however; so let us hope that the necessary data will become available.

DISABLEMENTS BY INDUSTRY

An analysis by industry is possible only for three broad industrial classifications: manufacturing, construction, and all other.

Of the three, construction is by far the most dangerous. If our cohort of 20-year-olds works in New York, it will experience two and a half times as many job-connected serious, permanent disablements in construction as in manufacturing; and three and a half times as many as in the "all other" group. This relationship exists at virtually the same level in each age category (Table D.2.). It also exists in New Jersey.

DISABLEMENTS BY AGE

The New York age-specific rates for deaths plus disablements show a slow but steady rise with advancing age. In New Jersey there is somewhat more fluctuation from age to age, but in this state also, the trend is upward with increasing age (Table D.1.).

In manufacturing the age-specific disablement rates (excluding deaths) rise fairly regularly with increasing age in both New York City and the State of New Jersey. But in construction there seems to be little consistent change with increasing age in either area. In the remaining major industry of the "all other" group there are pronounced increases (with advancing age) in the age-specific rates in New York City; in New Jersey, however, there appears to be no consistent relationship between age and level of injury rate (Table D.2.).

This question of the possible relationship between age and rate of serious injury is of great importance, particularly from the viewpoint of hiring older workers. Our data are inconclusive since we could not separate out injuries which may be concomitants of aging as much as of the job. For example, an accident which would not result in a permanent serious injury if it occurred to a 25-year-old man might be much more serious if experienced by a 45-year-old man. The disablement of the younger man would, therefore, not enter into our statistics, while that of the older man would. Detailed examination of the records of the workmen's compensation files, however, would probably go far toward separating such injuries associated with aging from injuries that clearly result from the job.

In short, many more data from the files of the various workmen's com-

173

pensation agencies, and analyses of these data, are needed before we can say with any degree of certainty what the relationship is between age of worker and incidence and severity of injury.

RESEARCH REQUIRED

Efforts should be made to obtain tabulations from several state agencies showing the numbers of cases by severity of injury, by industry of occurrence, by age and sex, and, if possible, by injury order—i.e., by whether it is a first, second, third, etc. injury. Separate tables can then be calculated for various industries showing the total number of injuries which a cohort will experience, and the probability of an individual worker's receiving an injury resulting in death or permanent total disability, a specific degree of permanent disability, and temporary disability, by degree of severity. If tabulations should become available it would also be possible to calculate probability tables showing the chances of a man's suffering any particular type of injury, such as the loss of an arm, a back injury, etc. Such tables can be related to the working force life tables published by the Bureau of Labor Statistics.

To the best of our knowledge no such tables have been constructed. At any rate, we have not been able to locate any.

Furthermore, it would be highly desirable to have such injury statistics for time periods which coincide with population censuses in order to have improved population bases. This would require the Bureau of the Census to provide additional tabulations showing detailed industry by class of worker by age and by sex, for states. Such tabulations are not now available (to the best of our knowledge), even though they would be useful for analyzing unemployment insurance as well as workmen's compensation data.

TABLE D. 1.

ESTIMATED NUMBER OF JOB-CONNECTED DEATHS AND SERIOUS, PERMANENT DISABLEMENTS OCCURRING BETWEEN AGE 20 AND AGE 50 PER 100 MALES EMPLOYED IN NON-AGRICULTURE

Age	Est. no. male em- ployees	No. W.C. deaths & ser. perm. disable- ments	Rate	Life table pop.			No. alive at beginning of age interval	Injury rate
	(000)		$b \div a$	L_x	(c)(d)	T_x	l_x	$f \div g$
	(a)	(b)	(c)	(d)^1	(e)	(f)^2	(g)	(h)^3

New York City*

20-24	172	196	.00114	497,645	567	4140	100,000	4.1
25-29	250	307	.00123	493,100	607	3573	99,058	3.6
30-34	281	365	.00130	488,345	635	2966	98,182	3.0
35-39	285	398	.00140	482,165	675	2331	97,156	2.4
40-44	277	453	.00164	472,900	776	1656	95,710	1.7
45-49	250	479	.00192	485,505	880	880	93,450	0.9

New Jersey**

	(a)	(b)	(c)	(d)	(e)	(f)	(g)	(h)
20-24	88	94	.00107	497,645	532	3674	100,000	3.7
25-29	131	158	.00121	493,100	597	3142	99,058	3.2
30-34	164	187	.00114	488,345	557	2545	98,182	2.6
35-39	164	238	.00145	482,165	699	1938	97,156	2.0
40-44	168	227	.00135	472,900	638	1289	95,710	1.3
45-49	151	215	.00142	458,505	651	651	93,450	0.7

* Including Westchester and Nassau Counties. Workmen's compensation cases closed in 1957. Most of these deaths and disablements occurred in 1955 and 1956.

** Workmen's compensation cases closed in 1956. Most of these deaths and disablements occurred in 1955.

1 National Office of Vital Statistics, *Abridged Life Tables: United States, 1957,* Vital Statistics—Special Reports, National Summaries, Vol. 50, No. 9, July 28, 1959.

2 Number of workmen's compensation deaths and serious, permanent disablements in each specified year of age and all succeeding years of age.

3 Number of workmen's compensation deaths and serious, permanent disablements occurring between specified age and age 50 per 100 males employed in non-agriculture.

175

Disabled Workers in the Labor Market

TABLE D. 2.

ESTIMATED NUMBER OF JOB-CONNECTED SERIOUS, PERMANENT
DISABLEMENTS OCCURRING BETWEEN AGE 20 AND AGE 50
PER 100 MALES EMPLOYED IN NONAGRICULTURE,
BY INDUSTRIAL CLASSIFICATION

INJURIES ONLY

	Age-Specific Rates				Injury Rates per 100 Employees			
Age	Total	Mfg.	Const.	All Other	Total	Mfg.	Const.	All Other
			New York City*					
20-24	.00105	.00140	.00200	.00072	3.8	4.4	10.3	2.8
25-29	.00116	.00146	.00350	.00076	3.3	3.7	9.4	2.4
30-34	.00123	.00136	.00394	.00089	2.8	3.0	7.7	2.1
35-39	.00128	.00148	.00355	.00095	2.2	2.4	5.8	1.7
40-44	.00150	.00173	.00440	.00110	1.6	1.7	4.1	1.2
45-49	.00169	.00173	.00410	.00138	0.8	0.8	2.0	0.7
			New Jersey*					
20-24	.00101	.00098	.00300	.00065	3.4	3.3	8.6	2.4
25-29	.00110	.00097	.00318	.00085	2.9	2.8	7.2	2.1
30-34	.00111	.00104	.00243	.00078	2.4	2.3	5.7	1.7
35-39	.00137	.00126	.00364	.00103	1.9	1.8	4.5	1.3
40-44	.00121	.00123	.00229	.00085	1.2	1.2	2.7	0.8
45-49	.00126	.00130	.00333	.00079	0.6	0.6	1.6	0.4

* See footnotes, Table D.1.

176

APPENDIX E*

RE-EMPOYMENT OF THE PHYSICALLY DISABLED: A BRIEF REVIEW OF THE RESEARCH LITERATURE

In a modern industrial economy it is impossible for most firms to hire workers on the basis of purely individual criteria. A solution to this problem is usually sought in categorizing applicants on the basis of such criteria as age, sex, schooling, physique, race, and experience. One consequence of this is to place certain groups at a disadvantage in the labor market.

Anyone at such a disadvantage—for whatever reason—is a potential cost to himself and his family, to his community and his society. As this cost is both economic and emotional, it is to be understood in qualitative as well as quantitative terms.

Ideally, a study of any such disadvantaged group would encompass the whole of that group's experiences, for the character of each experience must to some extent influence that of the others. But the sheer size of such a task suggests that if progress is to be made in this field it will best come from the steady accretion of findings from studies which concentrate on only one or a few aspects of the larger problem. It is in this spirit that we have undertaken our own research.

Our focus in this paper will be on the job experiences of one such dis-

---

* This appendix originally appeared as Exhibit C, "Re-Employment of the Physically Disabled: A Brief Review of the Research Literature," by Lincoln H. Day, in *Research Conference on Workmen's Compensation and Vocational Rehabilitation, 1960*, edited by A. J. Jaffe. New York: Bureau of Applied Social Research, Columbia University, 1961. Numbers in parentheses refer to references at end of Appendix.

advantaged group: the physically handicapped.* It will be obvious that we have not covered all the literature on this topic, even as it has been narrowed down for our study. But we do feel that we have covered most of the available recent literature which seemed directly relevant.

Little is known about the re-employment of persons who have become permanently disabled as the result of job-connected injuries. In fact, little is known about either the employment or re-employment of the disabled in general, regardless of the origin of their disabilities. What information there is comes largely from studies undertaken for purposes other than the study of employment. The utility of these findings is limited by such things as small sample size, the failure to separate men from women (a serious limitation in labor market studies), non-random selection of cases, or failure to separate by nature of injury or severity of disability. This failure to separate by nature of injury or severity of disability is particularly limiting to any study of rehabilitation because of the likelihood that only the most seriously disabled require such a program.

The very limited data available suggest the following concerning the re-employment of those who have suffered job-connected disablement:

1. *Self-Employment*

In the California study (1, Table 9) .5 percent of the 8041 expected to return to former employment reported that they were self-employed within 80 days after injury. Of the same group 6 to 9 months after injury, supplemented by an estimate of the distribution of those who did not reply to the questionnaire, only 1 percent were found to have gone into business for themselves.

It is generally assumed that lump sum settlements are made to enable the recipient to undertake a rehabilitation program or to start a business. Yet a Michigan study (4) of lump sum beneficiaries 12 to 18 months after injury found that only 4 percent had used any of their benefits to start their own businesses.

A follow-up study of 531 clients (one-third of whom were women) who had received rehabilitation services at a clinic in New York City (2) found that 7 percent of those who had received rehabilitation 10-11 years before were self-employed at the time of interview, while 10 per-

---

* We shall omit from this summary certain research areas related but not directly central to our main problems, such as sheltered work shops, vocational studies, medical studies regarding the physical abilities of disabled persons, psychological studies on "accident proneness," etc.

cent were self-employed from among the remainder, made up of persons who had received rehabilitation only 2-4 years before interview. As this sample included very few who were disabled as the result of job-connected injuries, it is unlikely that the high percentages self-employed are indicative of the employment experience of those with job-connected disabilities.

By contast, a Missouri study (6) of 495 seriously injured workmen's compensation recipients who underwent physical rehabilitation after 1951 found only 2 percent who had gone into business for themselves.

2. Rehabilitation

Because of the failure of the various studies to distinguish cases by nature of injury or severity of disability, it is not known what proportion of those seriously enough disabled to *need* rehabilitation actually fail to get it. Nor is it known what proportion of those who take *vocational* rehabilitation ever use what they have learned. But on the basis of the very limited materials available it appears that few of those with job-connected disabilities undertake rehabilitation. It also appears that most of those who do undertake rehabilitation are disabled for reasons not connected with employment.

For example, although the Michigan study (4, p. 5) does not discuss rehabilitation directly, it does note that only 6 percent of those who received lump sum settlements "used any of the fund for vocational rehabilitation purposes such as starting a business or buying a farm or securing additional training."

A national survey of 10,000 deaf persons, nearly all of whom were whites between the ages of 20 and 39 (3), found that most of those who had studied a trade had never followed it.

A follow-up study of all persons who had undertaken rehabilitation at a New York rehabilitation center in 1940-41 and 1948-49 (2) reported a distribution of disabilities of which no more than 15 percent could have been job-connected. Had the actual proportion been reported, it is likely that the percentage would have been much less.

3. Re-employment

Return to work is particularly difficult to determine with any certainty from the materials currently available. It is here that the limitations already listed are at their most frustrating: the failure to distinguish between men and women, the non-random selection of cases, and the failure

179

to distinguish by nature of injury or severity of disability are not calculated to illumine dark corners in any study of employment.

One study (1) reported that just over half of the industrially injured workers who were expected to return to former employment were actually working 6-9 months after disablement. What happened to those who were not expected to return to their former employments was not reported.

Another study (2) found 41 percent with jobs 2-4 years after rehabilitation and 71 percent with jobs 10-11 years after. But the limitations arising from a failure to separate by sex are illustrated by the fact that housewives comprised 6 percent of the more recent group and 12 percent of the earlier. As the two groups were unequal with respect to disability, a comparison of the percentages who had returned to work is of little value.

The Michigan study (4, 5) found that about one-third of the married men (single men were excluded from this particular set of statistics) had returned to work within a year of disablement. However, some 40 percent of them were still out of work 13-21 months after the settlement of their workmen's compensation cases.

Among 385 Missouri workers disabled on the job, 69 percent had returned to work within 60-90 days of their completion of a physical rehabilitation program (6).

4. *Post-Injury Job Characteristics*

Only two of the studies cited had any information on this topic. Despite differences in the composition of their samples, there was considerable agreement between them. One reported approximately 70 percent of the employed back at work with the same employer (1); the other reported approximately 87 percent (6). Both reported approximately 90 percent receiving the same or a higher rate of pay; and both reported approximately 70 percent engaged in the same kind of work.

This is in some contrast to a study of orthopedically disabled men during the 1917-1930 period (11). In this study it was found that the number employed after disablement increased 24 percent in the unskilled category and 6 percent in the clerical; while there were declines of 11 percent in the proportion employed in semiskilled and 19 percent in the proportion employed in skilled jobs.

180

5. *Attitudes of Employers Toward Hiring the Physically Handicapped*

It is not known for certain to what extent the re-employment of injured workers is determined by their own abilities, and to what extent it is determined by the attitude of employers. According to Barker (10), "The consensus of studies made . . . during the 1930's and 1940's was that 20% to 50% of employers did not, as a matter of policy, employ workers with appreciable physical disabilities except where the labor market was tight, as in wartime" (12, 15, 16, 17).

A later study (13) of 185 large concerns found 44 percent with fewer than 20 disabled persons in their employ, 43 percent giving employ- ment only to certain classes of the disabled, and only 13 percent with a definite policy of not excluding an applicant because of a physical impairment.

A study of hiring policies and practices in New Haven, Connecticut, and Charlotte, North Carolina (14) "found that the employment policies of the industrial managers by no means reflected their personal choices. Hiring policies were determined to a very large extent by the nature of the problems and the tasks that the employers faced and by the com- pulsions placed on them by their roles in society." The qualifications thought to be of "outstanding importance" in hiring good workers were such as the following: character, sex, personality, physique, experience, education, color, age, etc. Physique was considered to be of "outstanding importance" by 51 percent of the New Haven employers and 68 percent of the Charlotte employers.

Noland and Bakke conclude that "Employers do not have as their *primary* (italics in original) goal the provision of equality of opportunity. . . . A general tightness of the labor market is perhaps the chief legiti- mate, and the only automatic, persuasive situation which can be applied to urge employers to take on the less employable people."

Two more recent studies (7, 8) lend support to the conclusions of these earlier studies. It was found that as of 1956-57 the large majority of firms in New York City had not knowingly hired disabled applicants in the year preceding the interview. The highest proportion reported was for firms with 500 or more employees; but even here only 37 percent had knowingly hired a disabled person. Just as a "tight labor market" favored the hiring of the disabled in New Haven and Charlotte, so it also favored the hiring of the disabled in New York (7).

181

Disabled Workers in the Labor Market

Only about one-third of the personnel officers interviewed in an exploratory study conducted in New Jersey and Iowa (8) reported that they had knowingly hired disabled applicants during the 12 months preceding the interview. Few in either state said that as a matter of policy they excluded persons with orthopedic handicaps, and there were correspondingly few who refused to hire persons blind in one eye. However, most of the personnel officers asked about it were reluctant to hire a person known to have a back condition.

Slightly similar results are to be found in some calculations we have made. These show that the New York State Employment Service, which placed 19 percent of the 4,385 physically disabled who applied to it in 1954, was able to place only 14 percent of the 274 hernia and back cases who applied. Placement of orthopedic cases, however, were merely at the average: 19 percent.

A third dimension to the hiring or not hiring of the physically handicapped was found in a study of 109 plants employing 11,000 physically impaired and 18,000 matched unimpaired workers. (9). It was reported that ". . . a sort of unconscious distinction [exists] between the person who has acquired an impairment after entering the service of the company and the impaired applicant seeking employment. It is more than a sense of responsibility to the impaired employee, although that is a factor. The employee who becomes impaired in the company's service is a good man who, perhaps, has to be put on somewhat different work. The impaired applicant, on the other hand, is an untried person who presents an immediate problem of placement."

It is, of course, quite possible that the important variable in this study was not so much the attitudes of the various personnel officers as the extent to which these officers had control over hiring and firing. In some industries, printing, for example, this is something handled almost entirely by unions. In others, unions may exert considerable pressure on firms to retain workers disabled on the job.

In sum, on the basis of the studies we have reviewed, it can be noted that employers are generally reluctant to hire the physically handicapped. They are less reluctant in a "tight labor market," however; and their reluctance is greater for some disabilities than for others. Moreover, they are seemingly less reluctant to re-hire a person who was disabled in their employ. Despite numerous rationalizations offered by personnel officers for hiring or not hiring physically handicapped applicants (7), hardly

182

any of them have had enough experience with this category of worker to know with much certainty what to expect from employing them.

Our knowledge is still very limited, however. These general findings we have reviewed are of only partial use. We need much more research to pinpoint who is and who is not more readily re-employed, to determine the relative importance of age, schooling, and type of disability, for example, and to determine the characteristics of the firms and personnel officers who are more or less likely to hire the physically handicapped.

STUDIES REFERRED TO:

1. California State Department of Education, *Progress Report of Special Research Project on Rehabilitation of Industrially Injured Workers Covering the Period of March 12, 1956 to September 30, 1958*. California State Department of Education, Vocational Rehabilitation Service, Industrially Injured Project, December 13, 1958. 60 pp. with tables. Mimeographed.

2. Marion S. Lesser and Robert C. Darling, "Factors Prognostic for Vocational Rehabilitation among the Physically Handicapped," *Archives of Physical Medicine and Rehabilitation*, vol. 34, February 1953, pp. 73-81.

3. Anders S. Lunde and Stanley K. Bigman, Summary of report, entitled *Occupational Conditions among the Deaf*, Washington, D.C., Office of Vocational Rehabilitation, July 1960. 7 pp. Mimeographed.

4. James N. Morgan, Marvin Snider, and Marion G. Sobol, *Highlights from a Study of Lump Sum Redemption Settlements and Rehabilitation—A Study of Workmen's Compensation in Michigan*, Economic Behavior Program, Survey Research Center, University of Michigan, 1958. 28 pp.

5. James N. Morgan, Marvin Snider, and Marion G. Sobol, *Lump Sum Redemption Settlements and Rehabilitation—A Study of Workmen's Compensation in Michigan*, Survey Research Center, Institute for Social Research, University of Michigan, 1959. 151 pp.

6. Richard Rousselot, "The Missouri Workmen's Compensation and Rehabilitation Program," paper read at the 1959(?) annual meeting of the IAIABC. 9 pp. Mimeographed.

7. *Survey of Employers' Practices and Policies in the Hiring of Physically Impaired Workers.* Federation Employment and Guidance Service, New York, May 1959. 133 pp.

8. International Association of Industrial Accident Boards and Commissions, *Report of Subcommittee on Subsequent Injury Funds,* Forty-sixth Annual Convention, Edmonton, Alberta, August 21-25, 1960. 9 pp. plus tables and discussion by A. J. Jaffe. Mimeographed.

9. United States Bureau of Labor Statistics, *The Performance of Physically Impaired Workers in Manufacturing Industries* (Bull. 923, U. S. Department of Labor, 1948).

10. In addition to the nine sources above, findings from the following are referred to in: Roger G. Barker, et al., *Adjustment to Physical Handicap and Illness: A Survey of the Social Psychology of Physique and Disability.* Social Science Research Council Bulletin 55, Revised, New York, 1953.

11. R. N. Anderson, *The Disabled Man and His Vocational Adjustment,* N.Y., Institute for the Crippled and Disabled, 1932.

12. C. G. Bluett, "The Employer's Attitude towards Vocational Rehabilitation and Related Problems," *National Rehabilitation News,* 1942, 8, pp. 7-10.

13. M. D. Kossoris and H. S. Hammond, "World Performance of Physically Impaired Workers," *Monthly Labor Review,* 1948, 66, pp. 31-33.

14. E. W. Noland and E. W. Bakke, *Workers Wanted: A Study of Employers' Hiring Policies, Preferences, and Practices in New Haven and Charlotte.* N.Y., Harper and Brothers, 1949.

15. *Census and Industrial Survey of the Physically Handicapped in California.* California State Department of Educational Bulletin, 9, May 1935.

16. *Industrial Health Practices: A Report of a Survey of 2064 Industrial Establishments.* N.Y., National Association of Manufacturers, 1941.

17. *Workmen's Compensation Laws in Relation to Employment of the Physically Handicapped.* U.S. Office of Education Misc. Series 2152, revised. Washington, D.C., 1941.

APPENDIX F

EXHIBITS

We have limited the exhibits presented in this report to several letters and newspaper articles which were used to contact sample respondents, to acquaint them with the nature and objectives of the study, and to secure their cooperation in arranging an interview appointment.

In Appendix A, "Methodology," we have spoken of the difficulties we experienced in the field work. The exhibits, then, are relevant to problems encountered in a follow-up study concerned with occurrences, many of which took place several years earlier. Also, in most cases an interview on serious injuries and their consequences was disturbing to respondents. Since the sample preponderantly represented lower socioeconomic groups, most respondents were relatively unfamiliar with the methods and objectives of survey research. These had to be outlined simply, but in considerable detail. There were very few direct refusals to an interview request. However, repeated mailings (two of which are represented in the exhibits), plus phone calls or, in many instances, direct contacts, were necessary before we could obtain sufficient interviews to be representative of men in the survey area injured on the job. The press clippings were enclosed with the letters, and clearly persuaded many men of the importance of the project. Mrs. Roosevelt's endorsement of the study was extremely effective in obtaining interviews with men who had ignored earlier mailings.

EXHIBIT 1

NEW YORK WORLD-TELEGRAM AND SUN, THURSDAY, JANUARY 7, 1960

Help for Disabled

Columbia University's bureau of applied social research will interview nearly 2000 partially disabled workers as part of a study aimed at helping other disabled persons obtain employment, it was announced today. The study is being financed by a grant from the U.S. Department of Health, Education and Welfare.

EXHIBIT 2

MAGAZINE PAGE THREE

MY DAY

Willing To Work

ELEANOR ROOSEVELT

Not long ago a study being carried on by the Bureau of Applied Social Research in Columbia University was brought to my attention. One of the problems of particular interest is a study of workmen's compensation beneficiaries.

These people are receiving workmen's compensation and are under medical care for injuries received. In many cases they have had a rather difficult time, not only with their injuries but in getting their claims for compensation recognized. And, of course, they are naturally worried should anything occur that would make them uncertain as to what would happen to them in the future.

It is important, however, in the medical picture, that there should be more knowledge given directly by the beneficiaries in order that they themselves may be helped in various ways.

＊   ＊   ＊

The study is being financed by the U.S. Dept. of Health, Education and Welfare, Office of Rehabilitation, headed by Mary Sweitzer, and it will extend over a three-year period ending in 1962.

Other studies that have been made show that many employers do not care to hire disabled job applicants—even if it can be demonstrated that these applicants can perform adequately the work required:

Therefore, the ultimate aim of the present study is to get employers to employ people who have been handicapped. It is hoped that there will be increase in the hiring of the disabled, rather than putting them on relief.

The people conducting the study need case histories from impaired workers relating their employment and job experiences subsequent to their recovery and re-entry into the labor market. For this purpose the study group is interviewing nearly 2,000 men in the New York metropolitan area who have received serious and permanent injuries while on the job. Most of these people were injured approximately five years ago, and in the questionnaire being sent to them there are questions concerning their present work status, questions about jobs held at the time of their accidents and some concerning their present working or unemployed status. These questions—for the good of the study—must be answered honestly and fairly by those to whom they are sent.

＊   ＊   ＊

No one knows exactly how many such disabled persons there are in the U.S., but it is thought that the number runs into the millions. More knowledge of the situation might certainly help those already employed to obtain better jobs and also help others to overcome some of the difficulties that are now encountered.

The answers given to the research group on the questionnaires are being kept in complete confidence. Only mass statistics will be published, so no one should fear that personal data will be made public.

It is hoped, therefore, that the injured or handicapped people who are being interviewed will cooperate fully in order to benefit not only themselves but many others who may suffer the same fate and find it difficult to get jobs.

187

EXHIBIT 3

MRS. FRANKLIN D. ROOSEVELT
55 EAST 74TH STREET
NEW YORK CITY, 21, N. Y.

May 23, 1960

Dear Sir:

You may wonder why you are receiving a letter from me. I have long had an interest in the welfare of persons who have been injured or become ill, and so I am happy to be able to write you about a scientific research study concerned with this important matter.

As you probably know, modern universities are increasingly engaged in carrying on scientific research. This is one of their most important activities. Sometimes this research has no obviously practical value; and sometimes it has a great deal of practical importance - as in the case of research in medicine, for example.

Columbia University is currently conducting research concerned with the job experiences of men in the New York metropolitan area who have been granted workmen's compensation for injuries they received while working. This is the first time this subject has ever been studied. Such research has been needed for a long time. A great deal has been learned about the medical aspects of work-connected injuries and illnesses, but nothing is known about the job experiences of injured persons once they leave their doctor's care. How many go back to work for their old employers? How many get different kinds of jobs? How many never return to work? These represent the kind of questions this Columbia University study will attempt to answer. Through such a study it will be possible to make recommendations for improving the opportunities of all who have ever suffered injuries or illnesses.

In order for this study to be successful, it is very important that the Columbia University interviewers talk to <u>everyone</u> whose name they have. You are one of these important people. The success of this study depends upon your cooperation. I hope we can count on you.

Very sincerely yours,

Eleanor Roosevelt

188

EXHIBIT 4

Columbia University in the City of New York | *New York 25, N. Y.*

BUREAU OF APPLIED SOCIAL RESEARCH   605 WEST 115th STREET

December, 1960

Dear Sir:

Columbia University is making a study of the job experiences of workers who have had accidents or become sick while working. The project is described in the New York World-Telegram and Sun, and in the article by Mrs. Franklin D. Roosevelt which appeared in the New York Post.

No matter how slight or serious your injury or illness was, we would like to talk with you about your experiences. For this study to be successful we must have information about your work experiences and those of men like you. By talking to us you will be making an important contribution to the understanding of the problems of men who have been injured or become sick while working. Everything you tell us will be kept strictly confidential.

A staff member from Columbia University can call at your home when it is convenient for you. Or, if you like, you can come to Columbia University and talk with someone here instead of at your home. If you want to come to the University we will be happy to pay your carfare.

Please fill out the enclosed form, telling us when we may talk to you, and return it in the stamped self-addressed envelope. Or, if you want, call us on the telephone. The number is UNiversity 5-4000, extension 2154. Ask for Mr. Day.

We have already talked to many men. The information which you and the other men give us will be very important for helping all men who have had accidents or become sick while working. So please fill out the enclosed form and return it in the stamped envelope, or call us on the telephone, as soon as possible.

Thank you very much for your help.

Sincerely yours,

Lincoln H. Day
Research Associate

189

APPENDIX G
SELECTED PAGE REFERENCES
to authors and editors, publications, studies, and
organizations and agencies cited in this report

(Page references refer to pages in this present volume)

Accidents, Injuries and Health

Day, Lincoln H. "Some Illustrative Rate Tables on Seriously Disabling Work Injuries," in *Research Conference on Workmen's Compensation and Vocational Rehabilitation*, edited by A. J. Jaffe. (p. 171)

Gurin, Gerald, Sheila Feld, and Joseph Veroff. *Americans View Their Mental Health*. (p. 11)

National Office of Vital Statistics. *Abridged Life Tables: United States, 1957*. (p. 175)

National Safety Council. *Accident Facts, 1960 Edition*. (p. 2)

Simmons, Walt R. "The Matrix of Health, Manpower, and Age," in *Social and Psychological Aspects of Aging*, edited by Clark Tibbitts and Wilma Donahue. (p. 34)

U. S. Department of Health, Education, and Welfare. *Health Statistics*. (p. 170)

——, *National Health Survey*. (pp. 57, 163, 166, 167, 170)

——, *Vital Statistics of the United States, 1958*. (p. 150)

Census

U. S. Bureau of the Census, *Current Population Reports*. (p. 150)

U. S. Census of Population. *New York*, "Detailed Characteristics." (pp. 4, 30, 32, 33, 48)

Compensation

Berkowitz, Monroe. *Workmen's Compensation: The New Jersey Experience*. (pp. 8-9)

Longshoremen's and Harbor Workers' Compensation Act, as Amended 1956. (pp. 8-9)

New York State Workmen's Compensation Board. *Workmen's Compensation Law*. (pp. 8-9)

New York State Workmen's Compensation Board. *Workmen's Compensation Law, 1958-1959 Supplement*. (pp. 8-9)

Skolnik, Alfred M. "New Benchmarks in Workmen's Compensation," *Social Security Bulletin*. (p. 5)

Somers, Herman M. and Anne R. *Workmen's Compensation*. (p. 2)

State of New Jersey. *Workmen's Compensation Law Revised Statutes 1937, as Amended 1957*. (pp. 8-9)

U. S. Department of Labor, Bureau of Labor Standards. "State Workmen's Compensation Laws." (pp. 5, 8-9)

Education

Katz, Arnold, *Educational Attainment of Workers*. (p. 36)

Employment

Bluestone, Abraham. "Major Studies of Workers' Reasons for Job Choice," *Monthly Labor Review*. (p. 106)

Day, Lincoln H. "Re-employment of the Physically Disabled: A Brief Review of the Research Literature," in *Research Conference on Workmn's Compensation and Vocational Rehabilitation*, edited by A. J. Jaffe. (p. 177)

190

Federation Employment and Guidance Service. *Survey of Employers' Practices and Policies in the Hiring of Physically Impaired Workers*, (p. 110)

Jaffe, A. J., and J. R. Milavsky. "Unemployment, Retirement, and Pensions," in *Social and Psychological Aspects of Aging*, edited by Clark Tibbitts and Wilma Donahue. (p. 34)

"Job Pay Levels and Trends in 60 Labor Markets," *Monthly Labor Review*. (p. 46)

New York State Department of Labor. Earnings, discussed in various articles in *Labor Market Review*. (p. 46)

Parnes, Herbert S. *Research on Labor Mobility*. (pp. 106, 113)

Stein, Robert L., and Herman Travis. *Labor Force and Employment in 1960*. (p. 36)

Wagner, Tobias. *Selective Job Placement*. (p. 76)

Employment and Age

Federation Employment and Guidance Service. *Demonstration of Feasibility of Vocational Rehabilitation for Vocationally Handicapped Persons 60 Years of Age and Over*. (p. 76)

Tibbitts, Clark, and Wilma Donahue, editors. *Social and Psychological Aspects of Aging*. (pp. 34, 40)

Tibbitts, Clark, Arthur J. Noetzel, Jr., and Charles C. Gibbons. *Employment of the Older Worker: Two Papers and a Bibliography*. (p. 40)

Finances and Income

Bureau of Applied Social Research. *Benefits, Incomes and Expenditures of Unemployed Workers*. (p. 134)

David, Martin, James Morgan, Wilbur Cohen, and Harvey Brazer. *The Economic Position of Disabled Workers, and Their Future Prospects*. (p. 30)

Jaffe, A. J., Jeanne B. Anderson, Mabel Hopper, D. Staffler, and J. R. Milavsky. *Unemployment Benefits and Family Finances*. (p. 40)

Myers, John G. "Income Distribution and Economic Welfare in New York." (p. 39)

Industry

Automation Committee, Armour and Company, United Packinghouse Food and Allied Workers, AFL-CIO, and Amalgamated Meat Cutters and Butcher Workmen of North America, AFL-CIO. *Progress Report*. (p. 93)

New Jersey State Industrial Directory, Inc. *New Jersey Industrial Directory*. (p. 110)

New York State Department of Commerce. *Industrial Directory of New York State*. (p. 110)

"The Failure Record Through 1959," in *Statistical Abstract of the United States: 1961*. (p. 108)

Rehabilitation and Retraining

California State Department of Education. *The Vocational Rehabilitation of Industrially Injured Workers*. (pp. 63, 70)

"Response Is Slow in Job Retraining," *New York Times*. (p. 93)

Socializing

Minneapolis Star and Tribune. "The Minnesota Poll." (p. 128)

Schachter, Stanley. *The Psychology of Affiliation*. (p. 11)

Social Service

Community Council of Greater New York, Inc., Social Service Exchange. (p. 130)

191

DATE DUE

JAN 3 1 1975		
DEC 4 1976		
DEC 1 7 1976		
JAN 1 0 1980		
APR 1 1981		
DEC 1 8 1982		
MAY 2 9 1984		
GAYLORD		PRINTED IN U.S.A.